DEALER
An Autobiography

DEALER
An Autobiography

Jon Kregel
with **Verne Becker**

Foreword by *Les Carter*

BAKER BOOK HOUSE
Grand Rapids, Michigan 49516

ISBN: 0-8010-5287-4

Printed in the United States of America

Unless otherwise indicated, to protect identities, the names of prison inmates and individuals involved in drug dealings have been changed.

Contents

Foreword

Recently I spoke with a young man who had kicked the habit of cocaine abuse after being hooked on an assortment of drugs since his midteen years. He had wasted so much money and squandered so many career opportunities that his parents had finally let go of him. He was incorrigible, they said.

I asked this man what had made the difference. How after so much unsuccessful cajoling from family and friends had he been able to alter his lifestyle? Hospitalization had been tried, and failed. Many confrontations had taken place. Tough love had been used. But nothing had worked. Nothing. What got him over the hump?

The young man, now in his early thirties, beamed as he told me: "I made a friend with a man who accepted me as I am. He had been where I was. He knew how I hurt. He understood me like no one else ever had. And this man was a Christian. At first he didn't force Christ onto me, but he *showed* me Jesus' love. As time passed, I wanted what he had . . . that peace, that calm confidence, that freedom. So after many long talks and much sharing from my friend, I accepted Christ as my Savior and life hasn't been the same since."

Ultimately, drug users are a lonely lot. They may not always look lonely, but indeed they are. They're hungry for approval and acceptance. They want to belong. And most of all they want to feel significant. So to overcome the life patterns of the drug user, what is needed more than anything else is an uplifting word of encouragement from someone who understands, someone who's been there and who can say "Let's work on this together."

In Jon Kregel's account of his own history of drug abuse, you will learn how to find victory when all seems lost. Jon has been there. He shares many of his experiences in a way that can only be recounted by an "insider."

Abandoned by his parents at a very early age, adopted by a loving missionary couple, Jon seemingly had everything going for him as he found his niche as a sports hero. He had a strong Christian heritage to draw from, yet as he got caught in the fast crowd, he learned that even a young man grounded in a conservative lifestyle can stray. But he also found that when he hit bottom, seemingly all alone, the Lord was there. And the Lord had plans to use Jon to be a friend, to touch the lives of many who need Jesus Christ.

You will find inspiration as you learn how Jon handled his roller coaster lifestyle and finally learned to let Jesus Christ be Lord and Master. I commend this book to you with the hope that you will find a friend in Jon Kregel, a friend who will illustrate by his own life that the loneliness of the drug subculture can be overcome by fellowship with the Lord.

Les Carter, Ph.D.
Dallas, Texas

Prologue

Is this really happening? It seems almost unreal—but here I am, playing professional soccer—right fullback—for the New York Cosmos. We are battling the Washington Diplomats in their home stadium. It's a give-and-go play between me and Pele, the world's greatest soccer player. As I sprint down the right side of the field, Pele passes the ball to me from the left. Still keeping my stride, I send it back to him, then cut into the center to get into better scoring position. My pass to him is terrible, but he handles it effortlessly, maneuvers around the defender, and sets me up with a perfectly placed pass. I have a clear shot. Without really thinking, I kick toward the left corner of the goal. The ball neatly skips past the lunging goalie and into the net.

Always, when a goal is made, the scoring player is surrounded by his teammate. Now they are cheering and slapping *me* on the back! The roar of the crowd echoes in my ears. Even after being a soccer star in high school and college, where I scored dozens of goals, I can hardly believe what has just happened. I have just made my first goal as a professional soccer player. And I was assisted by Pele, the legend, the Babe Ruth of soccer. It seemed so easy—a couple of passes back and forth, a quick kick, and I had scored. Of course, Pele makes *every* soccer play look easy. Yet something is different about this goal: it represents a milestone in my life. I have always hoped to play pro soccer, but often wondered whether I'd actually be able to pull it off.

Now I have!

Not only has my dream of playing pro soccer come true, but I believe I will actually be a key player on this team. I'm in a career that uses my natural talent, and I know that in time I will be fully accepted by the other guys on the team. Once again I feel invincible!

What I *don't* know at this moment of victory is that my life is on its way down—deeper down than I could ever imagine. Ten years from now, the joy, the glamor, and the thrill of playing soccer will be but a distant memory, clouded by the dark events of a seemingly good life gone sour. How that could happen to a missionary kid from Spain who went to Bible college and has now made it big, I won't know for a long time.

One

A Mom and Dad at Last

*A small child, kicking around a small plastic
soccer ball in a Marburg, West Germany,
orphanage. The year is 1956, and that ball is my
favorite toy. I keep it all to myself. If the other
kids try to take it away, I hit them.*

*W*hen I was born three-and-a-half years ago,
my mother left me here at this *kinderheim*. But then she never came back, and
I am still waiting for her to come visit me. Lots of the
other kids get visited by their parents, but mine never
come. I wonder where they are, what they are like.
Why they don't seem to want me? I feel very angry at
them sometimes.

I get angry at the other kids, too. Fighting and making
trouble seem to be the only ways I can get attention.

Sometimes I'm able to lie my way out of it. But when I get caught, the housemaid punishes me by locking me in a dark closet until I have served my time.

One day a young couple shows up, wanting to see me. Their names are Harold and Esther Kregel, and they are from Spain—missionaries, I am told. They look at my wavy, unkempt reddish-blonde hair, my wrinkled, ragged clothes, and my suspicious eyes. Harold doesn't speak German, so Esther bends down and talks to me. I politely bow my head and shake hands, as German children are taught to do. There is something about the way they smile at me—something deep and genuine. *Could these people be my parents?* I wonder.

Before I can figure it out, however, they go away again. Several months go by, and they still don't come back. I'm confused. Shortly after my fourth birthday, someone at the orphanage explains to me that Mr. and Mrs. Kregel are going to adopt me. I will go live with them in Spain, and they will be my mommy and daddy. I'm not sure I understand, but I'm excited to learn I'm going to have my mom and dad at last.

The day for me to leave the orphanage finally comes, six months after my new parents' first visit. I cling to my soccer ball and stand by the door, awaiting their arrival. As their green Morris Minor pulls into the driveway, I am filled with excitement. The Kregels throw their arms around me, and I feel their love. They present me with a cuddly brown teddy bear, which I clutch tightly, along with my ball. I speak to my parents reverently, say good-bye to my dorm-mother (only at my new mom's request), and get into the car.

I adjust with great difficulty to my new home in Barcelona, the language barrier being a major problem; I can speak only to Mom, since Dad doesn't know German. But I don't like speaking German; my life there was so awful that I hate anything having to do with Germany, including its language. I want my parents to like me, but since I've never had parents before, I don't know how to act around them. Though Mom and Dad shower me with love and affection, I recoil. They give me lots of toys to play with, but I prefer my soccer ball from the orphanage and my teddy bear, and I carry them wherever I go. All I know about relating to people is fighting and making trouble.

At one point I get very sick. Extensive tests show nothing wrong with my health. Finally a pediatrician examines me. "Little Jon can't handle all the freedom you're giving him right now," he tells my parents. "He needs lots of structure, as well as firm, loving discipline." As Mom and Dad tighten up on me, I notice the difference and feel a little better. The structure seems more like what I was used to at the orphanage. But inside, under the surface, my anger and insecurity continue to fester.

I am more than a handful for my parents, who lead very busy lives as missionaries. Dad pastors a congregation outside of Barcelona, and must run back and forth to the church several times during the week. The old church has about three hundred members—small by United States standards, but large for Spain. Since Dad preaches and Mom plays the organ, I usually sit next to her on the organ bench.

When I'm old enough, my parents enroll me in the Swiss School of Barcelona, a German-speaking school. This frustrates me greatly, because I hate speaking German. I'd much rather learn one of the languages my parents speak—English or Spanish. So in the two years I attend this school, I rebel and make trouble in any way

I can. I ignore my schoolwork because it only makes me more angry inside. The school officials label me a "slow learner" and a "discipline problem."

After one exasperating day in second grade, my anger has risen to the boiling point. That evening, while Mom sits down with me on my bed to read a Bible story, something in me snaps. I jump up and start yelling at her: "Why did you leave me in the *kinderheim* all those years? How come all the other kids' parents visited them, but you never came to see me once?"

I am so furious that I run into the kitchen and grab a big knife off the counter. Then I threaten to use it to "get" Mom—and Dad, who has just arrived on the scene. We spend most of the night talking and crying and struggling. Mom and Dad explain to me that it wasn't they who left me in the orphanage, but my real mother. They tell me that they came to take me out of the *kinderheim* and into a real home where I can have loving parents to live with. That's what it means to be adopted, I hear.

Eventually my fury subsides, and I think I understand things a little better. Mom and Dad have told me before that they adopted me, but somehow I still can't get it through my head exactly what that means. There are so many unanswered questions: *If I am adopted now, what happens to my real parents? Why did my real mother leave me? Is there something wrong with me? Where is she now? And what about my dad? Where is he, and does he care about me? Why didn't they ever come back?*

Whenever I think about being left in that orphanage, I feel like there is a big, empty hole inside of me. And I don't know what to fill it with—except anger.

Later my parents are advised to take me out of the Swiss school because of the language association with

The Kregels—
Esther, Harold,
and young Jon.

Jon and sister Karen.

High school graduate
Jon, age 17.

15

my past history. Mom and Dad decide to enroll me in the Anglo-American School of Castelldefels, an English-speaking school. I will start there after the family returns from furlough in the States. Though I remain suspicious of school in general, I'm happy to be leaving the German language behind.

The highlight of our trip to the United States for me is when we stop in Chicago and Mom and Dad adopt a baby girl, Karen Eunice Kregel. I am so excited to have a baby sister. I recall many nights at my bedside when I prayed for God to send me a little sister. Now my prayers are answered.

I start fresh in my new school back in Spain. Each morning shortly after seven, a red school bus appears at the top of the hill and picks me up. I sit in the lone seat across from the driver, picturing myself as the proud co-pilot of that grand old bus. Together we navigate the streets of Barcelona, acquiring more kids along the way.

Once the bus fills up, we head south down the highway to Castelldefels, about twenty miles away. It is 9:00 A.M. when we pull up at the school, a small building at the intersection of two rarely traveled dirt roads. Giant pine trees and a white iron fence surround the three-story structure. Only a hundred yards down the road lie the white beaches and deep blue waters of the Mediterranean Sea.

The old building sports gloomy hallways painted dark green, creaky wooden stairs, and a tall principal who wears an eye patch. A large wooden paddle hangs on his office wall, ostensibly for decoration.

My favorite teacher is Mr. Annis, the science teacher, because he likes to experiment. We design a spectacular kite with a long tail, then stand on the beach and fly it

Jon attended this elementary school in Castelldefels, Spain.

Along the Costa Brava coast. The Kregel family spent many happy vacation hours in this area.

out over the Mediterranean. After claiming first prize for the highest and farthest-flying kite, I need more than an hour to reel it in.

After school each day I board the red bus again for the two-hour ride home. I am dropped off sometime between six and six-thirty—a long day indeed for an elementary school kid. Unfortunately, my work isn't over yet. I work on whatever homework I might have until bedtime, which is eight or a little after. My mom was usually home. I might see my dad before bed—or I might not.

Each morning I start the cycle all over again. As a kid—especially such an insecure one—it's hard for me not to have my father around more. Sometimes several evenings go by without my seeing him. Anger rises to the surface when at times I feel as though my parents care more about their work than they do about me.

I feel much better about Castelldefels than the Swiss school. I take a greater interest in my schoolwork, and get grades that are okay, except in math. I still get into trouble, though. One time someone reports me for throwing water balloons out of the bus window. Not only do I get walloped with the principal's paddle, but I am banned from recess for three months.

Many times during my years at Castelldefels, I take time out to walk along that Mediterranean beach and ponder the wildly divergent emotions of the sea—so calm and smooth on one day, so violent and explosive on another. Subconsciously I know these same conflicting emotions lie within me, and I am afraid.

The wind whips through my hair as I ride to church in the sidecar of my dad's Lambretta motor scooter. The church is in the town of Tarrasa, twenty miles north of Barcelona, and I take this trip with him every Sunday. I enjoy the ride even more as I get older, because I am allowed to sit right on the bike behind my dad, while Mom holds Karen in the sidecar.

Two

Invincible!

*Graduating from the Anglo-American School of
Castelldefels, and beginning ninth grade at the
American High School of Barcelona, back in the
city. Only fifty kids attend the school, about one
busload. Most of their parents work for Sears, the
American military, or the American Consulate.*

*I*n contrast to the rural, idyllic setting of my previous school, the high school occupies the fifth floor of an apartment building near downtown Barcelona. Vacant rooms serve as classrooms, and a centrally located unit functions as a student lounge, where kids study, sleep between classes, and sometimes dance to whatever music echoes up the stairwell from the apartments below. Though the facility certainly won't win any awards, I appreciate its location much closer to home, freeing up a lot of my time and allowing me to see my parents a little more often.

Besides a few teachers, two people (more likely, one and a half) run the school. Mr. Sozio, the balding principal, spends most of the school day at the neighborhood bar down the street. Despite his drinking problem, he takes a liking to me, and quickly appoints me to be his errand boy. Whenever his secretary, Miss Iris, has a question about anything, she sends me to the bar to extract a final decision from "Doc Sozio." Otherwise, she runs the show. I like the "privileged" position I have as Right Hand Man to the principal—it makes me feel important.

One teacher in particular impresses me as I begin high school: Ms. Beverton, English composition. A mere four-feet-ten, she has carrot-red hair, a crazy sense of humor, and she likes the way I write. Around her I sense I'm a worthwhile person, and she makes me feel that my papers are near-masterpieces. I always look forward to her class. Unfortunately, the approval of the principal and one teacher doesn't satisfy me. I still desperately want to be liked by the other kids, to feel that I fit in.

Since I've always been athletic, I focus my attention and energy on sports. Soccer—the Number One sport in Spain—is my favorite. But because our school is so small it has never had a soccer team. As a freshman, I immediately decide to change that.

After rounding up all the guys I know who can play soccer, we are still short of the eleven needed to make a team. So I turn to the girls and convince a few of the tough ones to fill out the roster. Then I talk one of the teachers into serving as our coach, though he knows nothing about soccer. He manages to arrange scrimmages and games with other schools, and the American High School soccer team is on its way.

We are an odd sight bursting out onto the field. Several girls play along with the guys, and we all wear mismatched uniforms. Meanwhile, our coach stands alone on the sidelines and cheers. Funny thing about our ragtag team, however—we always seem to end up on top, game after game. Since we have exactly eleven players, no one ever occupies the bench or has a substitute. If someone is sick or gets hurt, we play short. In one game we are forced to play the final minutes with only six players, but we still manage to win. Our team has winning records during all four of my high-school years.

When soccer season concludes each year, I join the basketball squad and play a major role in its conquest of the shorter Spanish teams. Whatever sport I play, it seems that I not only play well, but my team wins. I collect practically every award or trophy my school can give for athletic performance and sportsmanship. I begin to feel that I've found my niche in belonging to a team and being needed by the other teammates. When I play sports, people look up to me in respect. I feel more confident. And, as I acquire more "sports hardware," my confidence swells into a feeling of invincibility. *Can anyone,* I wonder, *beat me at anything?*

I yearn to have it all in my social life as well. I'm a star on the field, but I still feel insecure around my friends. I want to be liked as a person, not just as a jock or a poor missionary's kid. I want to be popular, to swerve into the fast lane, to hang over the edge.

Although I'm tempted to drink and smoke like so many of the other guys, I resist because I think I want to pursue a soccer career and don't want to mess up my body. Drugs aren't really an issue right now because no one seems to have them. In lieu of alcohol, drugs, and cigarettes, I choose to spend time with the "clever" troublemaking types—guys who have fun and live dangerously.

I have friends such as Bo, a big "tough guy" who likes me because I'm good in sports. His parents work for the international division of an American clothing store, providing him with an endless supply of cool outfits. For some reason his parents never seem to be home, and Bo sponsors party after party at his house. There's also Thor, a rich guy with long blonde hair who does whatever he wants and doesn't care what anyone thinks of him. While every guy in the school wants to date Doc Sozio's gorgeous daughter Maria, only the mighty Thor dares to ask her out. They quickly become a couple, and Thor earns the envy of all twenty of the rest of us guys. Another friend is Charlie, a fun-loving prankster who lives in a high-rise apartment building and also has money. These three guys, I decide, will be my ticket to fun, excitement, and faster living.

The four of us frequently go over to Charlie's after school, lock ourselves in his room, and play Led Zeppelin albums. Sometimes we pitch water balloons at passersby from his eighth-floor balcony. As our aim improves, we get bored with water and fill the balloons with more interesting substances, such as ketchup, mayonnaise, mustard, or whatever else we can find in the refrigerator. We wait for a perfect target—a man in a nice suit or a woman wearing a leather coat—and Bombs Away! Eggs, tomatoes, and other soft foods also serve as excellent artillery. Though we encounter a few close calls, we never get caught. I thrive on the "danger," the laughter, and the rush of adrenaline each time we make a direct hit and scramble for cover. Not getting caught reinforces my sense of invincibility.

Sometimes we go over to the amusement park, but I can't do much there without money. (The other guys always seem to have cash whenever they need it.) So one afternoon while my parents are down in the bookstore, I sneak into their room and steal a few hundred *pesetas* (five or six dollars) from Dad's closet. Since they say nothing about missing any money, I assume I can get away with it—like I do with everything else. I continue to pilfer some spending money each week.

Three

Testing Love's Patience

Living dangerously and bumping up against the law for the first time at age fifteen. While snooping for money in my parents' room one afternoon, I spot the beautiful buck knife Dad uses when we go camping. It is from Albacete, the knife capital of the world, and has horsehair casing and a four-inch stainless steel blade.

I know the knife will impress the guys at school, so I stuff it into my pocket. Sure enough, when I produce the knife the next day at school, they love it. Carefully they take turns snapping it open and striking threatening poses, while the sun glints off the blade. I am the hit of the day. After school Bo, Thor, Charlie, and I take our usual jaunt over to Charlie's. At one of the street corners a car flies by so fast and so close to us that our clothes flap. Still high from the day's *coup*, I decide to teach the next car a lesson.

"Hey, guys," I announce as I pull the knife from my pocket. "I'll bet I can get these cars to slow down and move over—watch." I drop my books and open the knife. As a car approaches, I jump out into the street and flash the blade at the driver, slowly at first, then rapidly back and forth as he draws near. I also shout tough-sounding warnings to the car as it passes. We turn away, laughing, only to hear brakes screech behind us. I look back. All four doors of the car fly open, and out jump four gray-suited police officers, all with rifles.

These are not ordinary cops, but specially trained riot police who clash with crowds and terrorists. I have watched these guys operate on the TV news, because riots have been occurring lately at the university. For a brief moment I refuse to believe that these men are after *us*. In the next moment, however, they march toward us, wearing gray helmets and dark frowns. Three of them grab Bo, Thor, and Charlie, while the fourth points his rifle at me. I am petrified.

"Toss the knife on the ground before you get into worse trouble," the guard says. Immediately I drop the knife and step back. His face falters for a second, still wondering whether he should continue covering me with his rifle. Then he relaxes a little and orders me to lean up against his car with my arms extended. I quickly cooperate, standing very still while he searches me. My body itches all over with fear, but I dare not flinch.

The guard drills me with question after question. "What is your name? Where do you live? Where did you get this knife? Where do you go to school? What were you trying to do in the street?" Then he and the other three officers step aside to confer. I look over at my buddies and see terror in their eyes. I tremble with fear myself. *What are they talking about?* I wonder. *What will happen to me? Will they take us all away? Will I go to jail? Will my parents have to come and get me out? Why are they talking so long? Oh, man, I can't believe this is happening!*

Finally the men turn toward us. One of them says, "We should be taking you to jail. But this time we've decided to let you go." I close my eyes and sigh with relief.

With the guard's next words, however, my relief vanishes. "We are going to keep the knife, however, and call your parents so they can claim it at the police station." At age fifteen, the thought of my parents finding out scares me far worse than even going to jail. Before I can catch myself, I blurt out, "Please, sir, isn't there another way we can resolve this?" *Oh, boy, now I've done it,* I realize. *I've narrowly escaped going to jail, and now I'm trying to bargain for more?* My face is flushed with anguish.

The policemen stare at me angrily. Finally one of them says, "If you don't like our decision, maybe you'd prefer to come with us to the station and do something about it." I decide not to take any more of the guards' time.

"No, that's okay," I reply nervously. "Uh, thanks for letting us go." *Please, please forget to call Mom and Dad,* I add to myself.

When I arrive home, I wonder if there's a way I can disconnect the phone. *No, that's ridiculous,* I argue, *they won't call my parents over a stupid knife.* That evening the apartment seems especially quiet; I stay in my room, unsuccessfully trying to do my homework. I tune my ears to the phone, praying that it won't ring.

It rings. The metallic bell pierces the silence, jolting my heart into my throat.

"I'll get it," I hear Dad announce. He lifts the receiver and says, "*Diga?* [Hello?]" Then a long, long silence, punctuated only by an occasional "Sí" or "Uh-huh." Eventually he says, "I'm very sorry for what happened. . . . Yes, that is our correct address. Thank you for calling."

Next I hear footsteps into the tiled kitchen where my mother is working. They talk, but I can't hear their words. Finally the inevitable summons is issued: "Jon, would you come in here, please?" My heart races, but I try to stay cool. "Be right there," I answer, shuffling a few papers to make it sound like I'm finishing math problems. Finally I peek around the refrigerator door nonchalantly. "You called?"

"Jon, have a seat—we want to talk to you," Dad says in his official voice. I know I'm in big trouble, but I can't bring myself to confess or say I'm sorry. Instead, I click into prisoner-of-war mode. Dad questions me for what seems like an hour, but I refuse to divulge any information.

"I want you to go back to your room," Dad finally concludes. "Wait there until I come to see you." More waiting. That's what really gets to me. I pace the floor, while time stands still. When Dad walks in, I'm sweating again.

Two of Dad's statements stand out as he removes his belt. The first is the standard phrase: "This is going to hurt me a lot more than it will hurt you." I get angry inside at these words—even more so as I receive the worst whipping of my life.

The second is, "Jon, we're punishing you because we love you." I pay little attention to these words as I cry myself to sleep that night, having been beaten and grounded for a week. For the next few days I don't talk to anyone in my family. But as life goes on, and I settle back into my same patterns with sports, friends, and stealing money from my parents, at times I find myself clinging to Dad's statement—". . . we love you."

I notice how much my parents pray for me. When I get up each morning, I usually find Mom kneeling next to the living room couch in prayer and Dad in the bedroom reading his Bible. They really have devoted their lives to God.

Whenever I see them pray for me or discipline me like Dad did for that knife incident, I know in my head that they really do love me. But they are always so busy with their ministry work that I often struggle with feelings of being unimportant to them—or at least less important than "The Ministry."

Four

School, Soccer, and a Wife

*Filing down the aisle of the auditorium, two by
two, carrying candles. I am at my high school
commencement, a part of the largest graduating
class ever—twenty. My dad offers the opening
prayer for the ceremony. I lead everyone in the
Pledge of Allegiance and later give one of the commencement addresses.*

*T*hat evening I have my first real date—a formal dinner party in a beautiful Barcelona
hotel. My date, wearing a long powder-blue
gown, and I join the other graduates in a huge ballroom
and sit at round, linen-covered tables. When I take her
home afterward, she thanks me for the nice evening and
gives me a soft, sweet kiss. For a minute, I think I'm in
love.

Preparing to leave for college in the States, I don't really know what I want to study. But since I know my parents want me to pursue biblical studies, I have agreed to attend a Bible school. I choose a three-year program at Grand Rapids School of Bible and Music, since I have relatives living in that area.

During the seven-hour flight to New York, and the much shorter trip to Grand Rapids, I wonder what Bible school will be like. I imagine a bunch of holy-looking nerds wearing prudish clothes, talking about God all the time, and seeking his "will" for every little thing they do. I worry over what I've gotten myself into, but my sense of adventure calms me down somewhat.

My relatives pick me up from the airport and weave through the Grand Rapids traffic to the small campus, which sits on top of a hill in the center of town. The main building is a four-story brick structure, painted gray. On one side, several old houses serve as guys' and girls' dorms; on the other stands a small chapel with a tall spire. Across the street lies a grassy empty lot where students can relax or play when weather permits.

The students, I am shocked and relieved to discover, do not appear to be a band of nerds. They are just normal people who believe in God, like me. I am hopeful about fitting in with this group.

Getting right down to business, which to me means trying to pull a soccer team together, I recruit mostly missionaries' kids and international students who have played lots of soccer in their home countries. At our first practice, three Africans, four Europeans, three Canadians, and a few others show up. Only one American appears, and he has no soccer experience, but since he plays good basketball, we appoint him as the goalie.

We manage to practice a few times before our first scrimmage. It is almost an instant replay of my high-school soccer team's first outing. Our uniforms don't match, our soccer balls are nearly flat, we run into each other because we don't yet have our signals straight, and we are badly out of shape. We lose the match, but leave the field fired up and determined to mold ourselves into a powerful team by the time the official season begins. Day in and day out, we practice, honing our skills, building our endurance, working out our plays. We scrape together enough money to buy uniforms and hire a trainer to wash them.

For our first game, we play Grand Rapids Baptist College, our school's biggest rival. They usually beat us in every other sport, and we vow not to let it happen in soccer. Nervously we scamper onto the field and the match begins. Both teams play a tight, close game, but when the final whistle blows, we have defeated our greatest foe 4–3—in our very first game. Victory is sweet, especially for me, since I score two of our goals.

In our entire first season, we lose only two games. Though we miss the play-offs, we solidify our team spirit and prepare for next year. My teammates become ten of the best friends I have ever had: Mark, Tim, Rick, Stephen, Jonathan, Clay, Larry, Steve, Ashad, and Mickey. Together the eleven of us work to put GRSBM on the map as one of the national collegiate soccer powers of the early 1970s.

In our second season, our team goes all the way to the national tournament for our division, losing only in the semifinals in Tennessee. As we win game after game, I realize our experience parallels that of my high-school team. We can't be stopped! Third year we breeze to an undefeated season, compete once again in the nationals in Indiana, and place third.

Not much in school matters to me but soccer. I manage to get by in my studies with a *B*– average, but soccer is my life, the ticket to my future as a professional athlete.

I smile at Peggy Dietz in the cafeteria line. She works in the kitchen of our dining hall and is a pastor's kid and a Christian Education major like me, though a year ahead. I ask her out, and we begin dating at the end of my freshman year.

The next fall I invite Peggy to my soccer games. She doesn't play sports herself, but enjoys watching me and the guys as we destroy our opponents. During the year we make room in our busy schedules to spend time together. We both attend classes all day. Peggy then goes to work in the kitchen straight through the dinner hours, and I go to soccer practice. Finally, at seven or eight at night, I am free to stop over at her dorm. Since the school rules forbid guys from entering girls' dorm rooms, we are only allowed to sit in a tiny foyer by the front door, which serves as a lounge of sorts.

Peggy's best friend, Judy, and her fiancé, Tim, usually join us as we hang out in the foyer. Since we don't have a car at first, we're unable to go out anywhere very often. Occasionally we make it to the bowling alley, or sometimes we walk over to Mr. Fables, a nearby hamburger joint, where we sit around, drink hot chocolate, and shoot the breeze.

My relationship with Peggy progresses in a very matter-of-fact way. Since I never dated in high school, and since my parents never explained the "facts of life" about love and marriage and sex to me, I have virtually no understanding about the process of falling in love. I assume that "love" happens when two people are attracted to each other, spend time together, and then decide to get married.

When Peggy and I can find the time and a place to be alone, we rarely if ever discuss our feelings, our needs, or our dreams. We neither explore the important issues in our lives nor take a hard look at our career plans. Occasionally we halfheartedly attempt to pray together, because we're told it's "the right thing" for a couple to do.

Mostly we make out. And, as our relationship gets more and more physical, somehow all those important issues we need to work out together don't seem to matter. One weekend, after visiting Peggy's parents, brothers, and sisters, I ask her to marry me. We set the wedding date for July, between my junior and senior year.

My dad performs a simple wedding in Peggy's hometown of Alpena, Michigan. The temperature soars to over 100°F, melting the film in some of the cameras of people waiting for us to exit the church. After a reception dinner, we open gifts and then leave for our honeymoon. We spend only a few days at the Holiday Inn in Grayling, Michigan, because we need to return to set up house in Grand Rapids before my senior year begins.

We rent the upstairs apartment of a house on Cherry Street owned by my grandmother. It has nasty green sculptured carpeting, but all in all it is a nice place. We pay only about $150 a month rent, and the house is about a block from the campus. We begin married life with little furniture other than a bed, some bookshelves, and a small stereo. Peggy continues to work in the school kitchen while I complete my studies and my last year of collegiate soccer.

I am happy, but between getting married and school and soccer, I feel as if my life is going too fast. Everything seems to blur together, making me wonder sometimes whether I'm in control of my life or whether life is controlling me.

I stand proudly at my graduation from GRSBM, then go forward to accept the Best Athlete award, the highest honor ever given to an athlete in the school's history. After our undefeated soccer season, I have already received most of the trophies and awards GRSBM can offer, as well as many from the Christian Collegiate Association of America. My living room looks like the trophy department at our local sports shop. Stepping down from the stage at my graduation, that strong feeling of invincibility again surges within me, crowding out what little dependence on God that I still feel. *No one can beat me*, I muse. *Not just in soccer, but in anything.*

Five

The Dream Unfolds

Automatically assuming that after graduation from Grand Rapids School of Bible and Music, Peggy and I will head off to the mission field. We never really discuss this in any depth; we just figure that people who graduate from Bible school go into missions.

*I*t doesn't matter that Peggy and I never once participated in the campus missionary organizations, or that we hardly ever went to church during my entire time in school. Soccer was the only school activity that mattered to me, and it took every bit of time that I wasn't spending with Peggy or doing homework. I couldn't have cared less about any Christian activities.

Still, we are proud to have completed our coursework, and we look forward to taking the next step of finding a position in the mission field. I don't really view my involvement in missions as an opportunity to bring the gospel to a hurting world, or any similar idea. To me it is just a job—one that I'm familiar with, since I belong to a missionary family.

I imagine everything working out like this: Peggy and I will write to my dad in Spain and tell him we're ready to join him and Mom in their ministry. They'll welcome us back to Spain and find something for us to do in their bookstore, or ask us to help with the youth group in their church. Because my parents have worked in Spain for so long, I reason, the mission board will accept us immediately since we are part of the family.

Memories of Barcelona dance through my head as I put together a letter to my dad. Peggy and I both sign it, and I drop it in the mail.

I stare at my dad's handwriting in disbelief. In his return letter he discourages us from coming to Spain as missionaries—mainly, he says, because my past behavior record doesn't look good. He tells us to find some kind of work here in the States for now, and that maybe down the road I can take another look at the mission field.

I am stunned at my father's response. I feel judged and rejected by him. *How can he do this to his own son?* I fume. *After I spend three years at the school he wanted me to attend, he then turns around and tells me to forget missionary work!* Dad doesn't know just how much his letter hurts me. (In fact, he won't know for many years.) But I am so angered by his seeming rejection of me that I make two decisions somewhere in my soul. One is to stop communicating with my parents. And the second is to scrap what little Christian faith I have and prove to Dad that I can make it in this world on my own, without him or his church or his God.

Riding through the darkness in Marvin's Fiat I'm about to try out for the Rochester Lancers, the farm team for the New York Cosmos of the North American Soccer League. I am tired, but I can't sleep in this little car. Besides, my mind is racing with excitement over what I am doing. Yes, I am bitter about Dad's barring Peggy and me from going back to Spain. But missions has never been something I really *wanted* to do with my life. Rather, it was something I thought I was supposed to do. On the other hand, I have dreamed of playing professional soccer ever since I was five years old. Not until now did I believe I would actually go after that dream.

I travel with Marvin, a guy I met who is also trying out for the team. To save money, we will drive all night on Thursday, practice with the team on Friday, Saturday, and Sunday, then race back to Grand Rapids, arriving Monday morning. That way we need to share a cheap hotel room for only two nights.

Tryouts are grueling, especially on top of all the driving. Marvin and I make the twelve-hour trip to Rochester four weekends out of the next six. Each time we return, exhausted, I try to assure Peggy that my prospects are good.

Finally it happens. I am notified that the Lancers have drafted me, and I am to report for practice in a few weeks. I am thrilled.

Peggy and I move our things to Rochester, and one of the people in management lets us rent the upstairs apartment in his house—a tiny flat with hardly enough room to sit down. After Peggy finds a job as a bank teller, we quickly relocate to a nicer townhouse. Before I know it, the season gets under way.

I move up from the Rochester farm team to the big-time, NASL New York Cosmos, after only a few months. Again Peggy and I pick up our things and look for another apartment. I can hardly believe that I now belong to a top-notch professional soccer team—a team with big-name players such as Franz Beckenbauer, Carlos Alberto, and Georgio Ghinallia. What's more, the team has recently signed on Pele, the greatest soccer player in the world.

Pele, whom I had watched and practically worshiped as a kid, was coaxed out of retirement with a three-year, multimillion-dollar contract and the opportunity to promote soccer in the United States. The realization that I will actually be playing on the same team with him dazzles me.

Shortly after I join the Cosmos, Pele arrives from Rio de Janeiro, Brazil, amid much fanfare. His contract with the Cosmos is such a big deal because, when he retired from the Brazil team in 1974, he vowed he would never play for anyone else. He had served his team, the Santos Football Club, for eighteen years and played in four World Cup tournaments. During those years he had become a national hero in Brazil and a worldwide soccer legend.

Now, only a year after "retirement," Pele has joined the Cosmos, much to the chagrin of his native country. On hearing about his contract, Brazilians are so enraged that they practically disown him. They tell him to take all his wealth out of the country and not come back. Their attitude saddens Pele, who simply wants to promote in the United States the game he loves so much. (I imagine that the money sure doesn't hurt, either.) Here he is welcomed as a demigod, though I notice he seems to shun the hero treatment.

Not long after Pele joins the team, we all arrive in Rochester for an away game with our arch-rivals in New York State, the Rochester Lancers (who have now become a full-fledged NASL team).

A press conference has been scheduled for Pele and the team at our hotel. We enter a makeshift press room packed with sportswriters, photographers, TV cameras and bright lights. Everyone wants to shake Pele's hand or take his picture. As the press conference is about to begin, someone finally realizes that Pele speaks no English. Since I am fluent in Spanish and know a little Portuguese as well, I step forward and offer to translate. The next thing I know, I am standing next to Pele at the podium, squinting at the glare of the floodlights.

From that moment on it is taken for granted that I will translate for Pele's press conferences until he learns English (I don't mind at all), and the two of us begin what turns out to be a great friendship.

Rooming with Pele for the first time while our team is on the road, I feel as nervous as if I have been told I'll be sharing a room with the President. I have idolized this soccer giant since I was a small boy—and now I get to be his roommate. I wonder how he'll behave in a one-on-one situation, without the rest of the team and the adoring crowds around him. I fret about how to act around him, but then tell myself how stupid I am to worry like this.

That night Pele immediately disarms all of my fears. He is a warm, kind, simple, fun-loving man who likes to do the same kind of crazy things that I do. For instance, at midnight that very night he decides to go out and get a pizza. I love the idea, so we wander the city streets and find a pizza joint that is still open. Once we get there, he discovers that he doesn't have any money with him and asks if I will pay this time.

Pele and I get along great right from the start, and we almost always room together when the team travels. I realize that he is one of the most genuine individuals I have ever met. It almost never occurs to me that he is a millionaire many times over. As I observe his down-to-earth, unassuming personality, I wonder how often that occurs to *him*. He treats everyone—rich or poor, famous or "ordinary"—with the same kindness and respect. And he expects to be treated just like any other person, never flaunting his money or indulging in all the excessive luxuries of wealth and fame. On the contrary, he rarely seems to have cash in his pocket and often asks me to lend him a quarter for a phone call or buy him a soda.

Pele's humility remains consistent even in public, despite the attention, adulation, and special treatment he receives. When fans stop him on the street, he takes all the time in the world to give autographs, talk about soccer, answer questions, or even kick a ball around.

The first time we arrive in Boston to play the Minutemen, a bus shows up at the hotel to take the team to the Boston College stadium for the game. Pele is told, however, that a limousine has been provided for him. Immediately he responds, "Unless you can get the rest of the team in that limousine, I'm not riding in it. I'm taking the bus."

I notice, too, that Pele doesn't feel or act like he's sacrificing a thing to be with the rest of us. He really enjoys it—even when it means cramming into the back of a taxi with six other guys to make it to the game on time. "I am here to promote soccer," he explains, "and I just want to be a part of this team."

I soon settle into the schedule, the excitement, the prestige and the lifestyle of being a pro. Soccer season begins in spring, breaks for the summer, and finishes up in the fall. The team plays between twelve and sixteen games, not counting scrimmages and exhibitions. Summers, we are free to play in summer leagues, join the staff at health clubs to stay in shape, and conduct soccer clinics.

During the season, we play all our games on Sunday. Monday is a day off. Tuesday, we assemble just to do stretching exercises. On Wednesday and Thursday, we pour it on for four hours of hard, grueling practice. Friday, we work on penalty kicks and setting up plays. On Saturday, we stretch and rest up for the Sunday game.

To an outsider, the schedule may not appear to be all that rigorous. Believe me, it is. In practice, the coach puts us through seemingly impossible, gut-wrenching drills. One of them is running up and down the stadium bleachers five or six times. First trip, we run up and down normally. We hop up and down on one foot for the second trip and on the other foot for the third. Fourth trip, we hop on both feet. The fifth trip is for running up and down with someone on our shoulders. On the sixth trip, we all change position so the riders now do the carrying.

It is forty-six rows to the top. And when we're all through, our sides aching, the coach says, "Okay, guys, good warm-up! Let's do the whole thing again!"

But traveling gets old after a while, too, as does play-ing in dramatically different weather conditions. Once, in Chicago, we play the Sting in Soldier Field, and it snows so hard we can't see from one end of the field to the other. Before long we can't find the white boundary lines; then we can hardly spot the soccer ball.

During half time, the referee comes into our locker room and informs us that there will be at least a half-hour delay while someone runs to the sporting goods store to buy an orange soccer ball for the second half. The ball finally arrives, but when we run out onto the field, we have to wait again while a guy clears the snow with a small lawn tractor. The field is a wet, slushy mess, and we all shiver, but somehow we end up winning the game, 2–1.

Sometimes I ride the bus with Pele through New York City. Two of his greatest loves are soccer and children, and his favorite off-season activity is for us to grab a soccer ball, hop on the bus, and watch for kids playing in one of the city parks. If we don't see any, we simply stay on the bus and let it rumble through its route again. When we eventually spot a few kids, we jump off the bus and offer to play soccer with them. As they discover they are playing with the one-and-only Pele, they run and tell their friends. In a matter of minutes, forty or fifty kids crowd around, and Pele and I organize informal drills and games.

Pele handles the kids with warmth, genuineness, and humility. He takes all the time in the world to give autographs, to answer questions, and to play soccer. If we don't happen to have a ball with us, he kicks whatever the kids can find. Or he'll step into the corner market next to the park and pick up a one-dollar roll of tin foil, and make a ball from that. Though the man is a millionaire many times over, he grew up playing street soccer in Brazil and never forgot how to "make do."

In addition to roaming the city streets, Pele and I conduct formal soccer clinics together in the New York City area and around the state in Syracuse, Rochester, and Buffalo. I thoroughly like working with the kids, and again I stand in awe as I watch Pele share his love for the sport, yet without succumbing to the trappings of hero worship. I marvel at how much he enjoys spending time with kids, and how friendly and creative he is with them. He seems to live for such moments.

We travel to California for two weeks of spring training during my first year. There we scrimmage with the Los Angeles Aztecs, and I meet singer Elton John, who owns that team. He is an avid soccer fan, and an excellent player in his own right; he joins right in the game and holds his own with the rest of the players.

Afterward he invites us all to his house for dinner, and we get a few glimpses of the inside. In one room, which is the size of an entire floor in an average house, he has covered all the walls with shelves displaying hundreds of sets of—what else?—eyeglasses. In his fully refinished "basement," there are two grand pianos—one bright white, and the other made of clear glass.

As the team travels, we have other opportunities to meet the rich and famous. In fact, several of the guys on the team are rich and famous themselves. Pele is a household word among soccer aficionados all over the world, and he is often stopped on the street for autographs. Most people agree he is the greatest soccer player who ever lived. He rakes in an annual salary of $1.2 million, and doesn't need one penny of the money. We also have Franz Beckenbauer of Germany's World Cup team, and Carlos Alberto, who previously played for three World Cup teams in Brazil; these guys receive hefty six-figure salaries.

Fighting to keep control of the ball in a tight play-off game with the Tampa Bay Rowdies, the score is dead even at 1–1, and there are only seconds left in the match. Valiantly we struggle to penetrate their defense and score a winning goal, but to no avail. The clock runs out, and the teams must now alternate taking penalty kicks to break the tie.

In this situation, we normally follow a prearranged kicking order set up by the coach. Three other guys go first, then I kick, and finally Pele takes the last shot, since he scores virtually every time.

First the Rowdies take their kicks, and score three out of five. Then it is our turn. Inexplicably, someone goes out of turn and messes up the order. Pele must kick fourth, and he easily ties the score again at 3–3. Then Coach Eddie Firmani tells me I have to shoot last—essentially placing the entire play-off game on my shoulders. If I make the shot, we win. If I miss, we start the whole tiebreaker over again, which could mean defeat.

After spotting the ball, I glance at the goalie for Tampa Bay and nervously survey my options. *Should I go for the upper-left corner or the lower right? Fake one way and go the other? Or assume he'll watch the edges and barrel it right down the middle?* Finally I stand back and set myself. The crowd quiets down, except for a few scattered yelps. I take a deep breath, then one, two, three, four steps to the ball and I connect.

The next two seconds go by in slow motion. I've made good, solid contact. The ball rockets toward the cage, rising higher and higher as it flies. When it nears the crossbar, it is just over shoulder high and barely inches out of reach of the straining goalie. It finally passes him and sinks into the net. *I've scored the winning goal!*

Everyone goes crazy—my teammates, the coach, the crowd. Even I do, as I am hugged and slapped and carried off the field and soaked in Gatorade. And I love every bit of it. I can't imagine life getting better than this.

As a soccer player, Pele is phenomenal beyond words—even at the age of thirty-five, which is old for pro soccer. He has such a scientific knowledge of the game, and superior skills to match it. If a soccer play requires that I be in a certain place on the field at a certain time to receive the ball, and Pele is doing the passing, I know absolutely that no matter what the other team's defense is doing, the ball will be there. Or if anyone passes the ball to him—whether to his feet or to his head or some other part of his body—Pele can not only control the ball, but also turn around and make something happen with it.

I have never in my life seen another player who comes even close to matching his skills. And this is in a league where a good percentage of the players are ages eighteen through twenty-five. Being eight to ten years older would put most players at a distinct disadvantage. Pele, however, not only has the skills to compete with these young stars, but he has the ability to make *them* look bad!

One might think that with such fantastic skills, Pele would be a one-man team out on the field. Here I see yet another aspect of his humility at work: he is a team player all the way. He makes plenty of goals on his own, believe me—but more often than not he sets up situations for others to score. He makes the rest of the team look great, and is willing to share the glory with the other guys.

Playing with Pele feels a lot like playing with a

revered teacher. I find myself studying his every move, learning everything I can about his techniques and his strategy. Occasionally, as we sit in the locker room during half-time, Coach Eddie Firmani issues a few suggestions to Pele. Inside I chuckle at this, since the coach doesn't know as much about the game as some of his players. Pele has every right to retort, "Hey, Coach, are you nuts or something?" Instead, Pele listens attentively, then says, "Okay, Coach—thanks." He wants to be a part of the team like everyone else, and that includes respecting the wishes of his coach.

During Pele's three years with the Cosmos, our team soars into first place. We win the league championship two years in a row, and in the third year we place second, losing in the finals to the Tampa Bay Rowdies.

Pele's humble approach to soccer—and to life— makes a profound impression on me. Though I have shelved Christianity myself, I find myself wondering from time to time if Pele is a Christian. I never hear him say anything to that effect, but he lives a life of such consistency, humility, and service to others that I think, *If I wanted to model my life after anyone, it would be him.*

Six

Conflicting Commitments

Living pretty well in New York on my salary,
depending on how bonuses and incentives work
out. Peggy and I have a nice townhouse in New
York, near the south end of the park.

*U*nlike many New York City dwellers, we own two cars. I drive a brown Grand Torino, which I've souped up with a big V-8 engine, mag wheels, and a custom paint job to look like a "Starsky and Hutch" car. Peggy drives an early-1960s-vintage Ford Falcon, which I bought mainly for its "antique" value. Peggy works full time for a nearby bank—and it's good she does, since we spend our money freely and don't save much.

Though I am having the time of my life pursuing a soccer career with the Cosmos, my marriage seems to be settling into mediocrity. Peggy and I don't have a lot to say to each other after work each day. When the team goes on the road, she rarely wants to travel with me except to an occasional game.

I am irresponsible. I think she resents that and all the fun I am having—"playing" for a living. Certainly professional soccer has plenty of perks, and the schedule isn't particularly heavy, but it takes a lot of hard work and rigorous practice to keep in shape and stay in sync as a team. I don't think she understands what a pro sports career requires of a person and I make no effort to understand her world.

On the other hand, I understand her disapproval of one aspect of my "playing": I tend to flirt with other girls a lot. In the sports circles I am a part of, there always seem to be plenty of cute girls around, and I admit that I enjoy being around them. Though at times I am tempted to go beyond the flirting stage, I don't do so. Still, I know Peggy doesn't appreciate my behavior.

The conflicts between Peggy and me are heating up. My soccer career and my irresponsibility are becoming more and more of an issue for her. It shows at the dinner table, where the following awkward conversation occurs again and again:

"So, how was your day, Jon?"

"Fine."

"What did you do?"

"Well, mostly I was just kicking around all day," I reply jokingly, even though I know it touches a nerve for Peggy.

Sure enough, it does, and the whole tone of the conversation changes. "That's all you do anyway," she retorts.

"Well, I happen to be feeding us and paying for this place," I shoot back.

Peggy counters: "You're sure not doing it very well—if I wasn't out there working we wouldn't be able to make ends meet."

We bicker back and forth until Peggy says, "Look, I don't want to discuss this any further unless we can talk about your going out and getting a real job."

A *real* job. Those words anger me above all the others, because I feel that they prove Peggy has no respect for my talent in soccer or for the dream I've always had of playing professionally. That dream has now come true, and she wants me to quit.

"Sorry, but I'm not ready to get a *real* job," I reply in defiance. "I'm doing just fine playing soccer."

"Well, you may end up having to play by yourself, then," she says. "You can play soccer or you can be married to me, but you can't do both."

It is a standard "argument," where neither party listens to the other, and both try to get in the last word. Eventually the artillery fire subsides, and one of us leaves the table. We spend the rest of the evening in different rooms, seething.

There's the pounding of forty-four feet up and down the field and the thud of bodies colliding to gain control of the ball. Today the grunting and grimacing of the players, the yelling and cheering fans, is in Meadowlands, New Jersey. It is just an exhibition game, but a very significant one: Pele's final game as a member of the New York Cosmos. And we are playing none other than the Santos Football Club, Pele's "home" team from Brazil.

We play an easy, low-key game, just for fun and to please the fans. At halftime, in a symbolic act of departure, Pele removes his Cosmos jersey, runs to the other side of the field and dons a Brazil jersey. He then plays the second half of the game for his native country.

I am nearly overwhelmed with emotion during the game, and especially afterward when the Cosmos put on a simple farewell ceremony. Pele and I have had such a great friendship, and I will miss him. Before he leaves the States, Pele gives me a special gift: a plaque that had been awarded to him by the NASL. The inscription reads, "Pele—in appreciation for what you've done for soccer in America." Pele signs the back of this plaque and tells me to keep it.

Peggy and I visit with some friends on July 4, 1976—the nation's Bicentennial celebration. Millions of people clog the streets of Manhattan for all the festivities, highlighted by the arrival of the Tall Ships—a noble caravan of clipper-type vessels that sail into the New York harbor.

We are mostly sitting around at our friends' place, following some of the TV coverage of the event and reading the newspaper. For some reason, that sore subject of soccer and work comes up between Peggy and me, and we get into an embarrassing argument right in front of our friends. Abruptly we leave and return to our own house.

I stand next to our living room window, looking out at the traffic. Then I turn to Peggy. "If you're so unhappy about my playing soccer," I say, "then why did you agree to move here in the first place?"

"I didn't know it would bother me back then," she replies. "But now I realize that this is what you are going to do with your life and there's nothing I can do about it. You've closed me out, and I'm unhappy with our life and with our marriage. I'm giving you a choice,

Jon," she continues. "It's either soccer or it's me, but not both. If you want to keep playing soccer, then I'm leaving. If you want to stay married to me, then you're going to have to find a job."

"Hey, wait a minute!" I protest. "That's not fair! If you really love me, you won't push me to make that kind of choice! Why does it have to be one or the other?"

Peggy remains unmoved. She has made statements to this effect before, but this time I realize she means it. She has issued me an ultimatum. Now I really do have to make a choice.

I communicate very infrequently with my parents, jotting off an occasional letter to them, but saying very little about what I am doing. Mom and Dad know that I am playing pro soccer, but I am afraid to tell them much about the soccer world. I don't know how they'll respond to the fact that I play soccer on Sundays and don't go to church. Sunday observation is a big deal in my family's religious tradition, and since my folks are so devout, I don't think they'll be able to handle it. Besides, I don't think *I* can handle any more rejection from them.

Now, as I consider the choice that lies before me, my parents come to mind again. If they'll be horrified to learn I don't attend church on Sundays, God only knows how they'll respond to the idea of my getting divorced. My parents and my relatives probably would turn their backs on my lifestyle.

A major conflict is waging inside me. On the one hand, I have rebelled against my parents on and off throughout my growing-up years. A big part of me doesn't give a rip about what they think. Whatever they say, I'll still go and do my own thing. After Dad told me not to come to Spain, I went right out on my own and got drafted by a pro soccer team.

But, on the other hand, my parents' values still exert a strong pull on me. I may skip Sunday church, but I feel real guilty about it. I may swear or may flirt with a girl, but sometimes a pang of remorse strikes me afterward. I may even consider getting divorced, but I know the guilt and shame will hang over me like a black cloud. As angry as I am at my parents, I'm not sure I can stand the stigma my family would place on me if I let Peggy leave.

The fact is, I think I really *do* want my marriage to survive. I just don't understand why I have to quit soccer for it to work. But Peggy's mind is made up, and she has given me a choice, which really amounts to no choice at all.

Seven

New Career, Old Problems

*Leaving the skyscrapers, the crowds, and the
excitement of New York behind. Even worse,
leaving behind the thrill of playing soccer with the
Cosmos, along with a lot of friends, national
recognition, and a big annual paycheck. Soccer
has always been my dream, and now I am
walking away from it.*

*W*hy am I doing this? Supposedly to save my troubled marriage. Or more accurately, to keep from getting divorced. Sure, I want my marriage to work, but more than that, I don't want it to fail. I'm too worried about what my parents and others will say. The stigma of divorce concerns me even more than working out my differences with Peggy.

When I tell her of my decision to quit soccer, Peggy is

very happy. She is hoping that this will be our chance to start fresh and live a "normal" married life—away from all the soccer jocks, away from all the traveling, away from all those girls. I try to show Peggy that I want our marriage to work, but underneath, I despise her for forcing me to leave soccer. Once again I feel anger welling up from deep within me. Though I won't consciously admit it, I intend to make Peggy pay for what she's done.

And what am I giving up my dream for? A rinky-dink job as aquatic director for a local YMCA in Indianapolis, Indiana. I have called a friend of mine who works for the Y, and he pulls a few strings to get me the job. The Y agrees to pay the expenses for us to move there. We find an apartment, Peggy gets another bank job, and I report for my first day of work.

I now view my job at the Y as temporary, because I have already decided to pursue nursing as my second career. After a year of attending dozens of swim meets, organizing swimming classes and scuba lessons, maintaining an indoor and outdoor pool, hiring and firing lifeguards, and attending endless staff meetings, I have had enough.

Enrolling in a special nursing program at Community Hospital, I work in the emergency room as a "tech" while studying for my degree. I enjoy receiving on-the-job training and learn quickly. Soon, in addition to my ER job, I join an ambulance team and study to be a paramedic.

My schedule is rigorous. During the day, I attend classes and study. Early in the evening, I work in ER, riding the ebb and flow of excitement. Sometimes it's so slow I can study or nap or socialize; other nights the room bulges with patients, all of whom need immediate help. Often I hop into an ambulance for a few late-night hours of on-the-scene emergencies. I thrive on the danger, the stress, the life-or-death responsibility. It's as if I get high on my own adrenaline.

Eventually I tire of the ambulance shift and, for the next three years, settle into a routine of daytime studies and evening ER work. When I come home at night—sometimes very late—every ounce of my energy is spent. And, around Peggy, I feel more and more empty. Our worlds seem to be drifting further and further apart.

I begin to stay out late to party with the other nurses. In contrast to the restraint I showed with other women in New York, I now find myself caring less and less about being faithful to Peggy. *I spend most of every day working and studying with these nurses,* I rationalize. *It's only fair that after an evening of stress in ER, I can socialize with them, too.* But I do more than socialize at these gatherings. I drink a lot and flirt shamelessly. Though Peggy resents my late-night frolicking, I ignore her.

At one party I'm attracted to a pretty EKG technician, and I begin seeing her on my off days. Before long we leap into a full-fledged affair, which I carefully conceal from Peggy. I have put myself in an awkward position. I don't want to lose Peggy, but my anger drives me to use other women to get back at her. I refuse to look at the underlying issues between us or try to work things out.

One day Peggy presents me with a card that has arrived in the mail. It is from my lover, and Peggy knows it. Having been exposed, I agree to cut off the affair. Surprisingly, Peggy says she won't leave. But I still won't let go of my anger at her. Then the last straw.

I find out my lover is pregnant and I'm expected to pay half of the abortion bill.

Halfheartedly, I attempt to patch things up with Peggy. At this point I don't think either one of us has the desire to put much effort into our marriage. We visit a local church a few times because a friend of ours plays the organ there. Peggy suggests that I meet with the pastor and get some counseling. Though I resent the implication that I'm the only one who needs the counseling, I agree to see him. When I arrive at the church, however, I am told that he is busy, so I leave.

Eventually Peggy and I decide to do the same thing many other young couples do when they find nothing but emptiness after a few years of marriage: have a baby. Planning for a new addition to the family temporarily rekindles a little warmth between Peggy and me. Together we shop for baby clothes and paraphernalia. We attack the second bedroom with paint and wallpaper, transforming it into a nursery. Wordlessly, we hope that perhaps this child will fill the void in our marriage.

The day of our child's birth unfortunately turns into a fiasco. In the morning I receive a call at school informing me that Peggy has gone into the hospital. When I call into work to explain that I need to be with my wife, they tell me that if I don't show up for work, I'll lose my job. I am furious, but I work my shift anyway and then rush over to St. Vincent's Hospital to see Peggy. There I learn that Peggy has given birth to a little boy whose name is Jeffrey.

When I first see Peggy, we promptly get into a fight. She's angry at me because I didn't show up at the hospital when she needed me. I'm angry at my employer for not giving me the day off. And now I'm also angry at

Peggy for not trying to understand the bind I was caught in. "Hey, you yanked me out of soccer and brought me all the way out here so I would get a job," I tell her. "And now you're mad at me for following my boss's orders! I just can't win, can I?"

As soon as I put my face up to the nursery window, however, my anger vanishes. There, in a Plexiglas crib, tightly wrapped in a little blue blanket, is an adorable baby boy with beautiful red hair. The rest of our time in the hospital, I gloat over Jeffrey being the best-looking kid in the nursery. I have so many plans for him, so much I want to give him. I'll teach him soccer and any other sport he wants to learn, and we'll play together and be the best of friends. I can't wait to watch him grow up.

After a few months, Peggy returns to her job at the bank, and I change my schedule so I can come home for dinner each day. I love my carrot-headed little boy. When I pick him up from the sitter after work, he smiles and squeals and kicks with delight at seeing his daddy. On my days off, I frequently bring Jeffrey to the hospital and show him off to the other staff. I am so proud of my son. Yet I begin to realize that even an adorable baby won't save our marriage. Except for the parental responsibilities I now share with Peggy, I feel no closer to her than I did before. The outside circumstances have changed, but the inner emptiness remains. I'm unable to get a grip on myself and figure out what to do. Somehow I have allowed my values and my sense of judgment to become clouded. And I continue to lie to Peggy. I can't be trusted.

I return to late-night partying with my nurse friends. The alcohol takes the edge off my depression, and the female attention makes me feel good. Again I lapse into sexual infidelity, sometimes not even discreetly. Deep down I know this lifestyle won't work, but in practice I live as if I can have it all—a wife, a child, girlfriends, parties, and money.

The snow is falling from the gray Indiana skies as I prepare to go home from my shift at the hospital. Just as I am about to leave, my replacement calls in sick, and I am asked to stay on for the evening. I call home to let Peggy know. No answer.

An hour later I try again, then another hour later. I worry that Peggy and Jeffrey went out in the Bronco and had an accident. At 9:00 P.M. I still get no answer and ask to leave early so I can make sure nothing is wrong.

As I pull my old Falcon into the snow-covered alley behind the house, I notice that the house is dark. There are no footprints in the snow. The door is locked. Fear grows within me as I move from room to room, looking for a note or some other clue as to where Peggy and Jeffrey might be.

The phone rings. I know it must be Peggy, but I'm afraid to answer because I feel sure I'm going to hear bad news. She got into an accident. Or something happened to Jeffrey. Maybe it's the police calling to tell me they've been killed.

It rings again and I answer. "Hello?"

"Jon—it's Peggy." Her voice is quivering, and she sounds stuffy, as if she has been crying.

"Peggy, where are you? Are you okay?" Worried as I am about their safety, I am not prepared for Peggy's answer.

"Jon, I am leaving you," she blurts out.

Peggy knows about my affairs, and I know she knows. Yet her words jolt my heart. "Wait a minute!" I say, panicking. "What do you mean you're leaving me?

Why? What about Jeff? What about all our stuff?" Tears well up in my eyes.

"I don't know about all that yet," she says flatly. "Look, Jeffrey and I are at my parents' house. We're just going to stay here for a while until I decide what I'm going to do. I'll let you know when we get back."

The call ends quickly. I listen for the click of her phone hanging up before I let myself cry. As the tears fall, I grow more and more bitter at Peggy. *This whole thing is her fault,* I tell myself. *If she were at home more instead of working, this wouldn't have happened. Who does she think she is? First she pulls me out of my soccer career and now she's running off with my son. What gives her the right?* I slam the wall with my fist in anger—at everyone except myself.

To keep myself busy and blot out some of the pain, I work incredibly long hours at the hospital that week, usually coming home only to sleep. Peggy and Jeffrey return, but she says nothing to me for the entire next week. I am too afraid to bring up the subject. Finally, one day after I arrive home from work, Peggy tells me she has made up her mind. She has met with an attorney and asked her to file divorce papers. Our five-year marriage is about to end.

Eight

Moving On

Looking up from my work at the hospital the next day. A deputy sheriff is approaching me. "State your name, please," he says. Bewildered, I answer, "Jon Kregel. Hey, what's this all about?" He then retrieves a batch of papers and a pen from his leather pouch. Handing them to me, he says, "Sign here."

*W*ithout even reading the papers, I sign. He tears off the top sheet, hands the rest to me and mutters, "Good luck." Then he turns and walks away.

I am standing in the hospital hallway. I look at the top line of the document. It says, in capital letters, JUDGMENT FOR DISSOLUTION OF MARRIAGE. Suddenly it hits me: I am about to lose the only thing that really means anything to me—my family. Again I feel the tears rising, so I dash into the men's room and weep out loud. Remorse, anger, shame, and fear all bubble to the surface, yet I still don't know what to do. Unless I go to court myself and contest the whole thing—which could turn into an ugly, nasty battle—I can do nothing to stop the divorce proceedings. I feel stuck.

Once my tears have run out, I leave the men's room and return, red-eyed, to my post. I don't feel at all like working, but I don't want to go home either. Since my shift is nearly over and I have cleaned and restocked my area, I finally decide to leave early. On the way out I bump into Deb, the head nurse on my shift.

"Hey, Jon," she says. "The party's at my house tonight—are you coming?" Deb is known for her wild parties. In my confused state, I think, *A party—just what I need right now. After a few shots of Wild Turkey, I'll forget everything.*

"Sure, I'll be there!" I tell her.

The party continues into the wee hours of the morning. By the time I'm ready to leave, I have given myself a good buzz from all the alcohol. I have also spent most of the evening with Nanci, a pretty blonde who is secretary to the ER doctors.

Driving around for an hour or two after the party, I try to muster up the courage to go home and face Peggy. It is nearly sunrise. I also wonder what I should do when I get there. Peggy and I have hardly spoken a word to each other about the divorce. We haven't made any arrangements or discussed how to divide up our property. I decide to let Peggy and Jeff have everything except my clothes and soccer paraphernalia. *That way,* I tell myself, *I can make a clean break and start fresh.*

Having made up my mind, I finally pull into the alley behind our duplex.

Inside, Peggy is already dressed and giving Jeff his breakfast. Her steel eyes tell me she knows where I've been, and that she's fed up. She leaves him sitting in his high chair and turns to me. "So—which one of us is moving out? And when is it going to happen?" she says coldly.

I can't really look her straight in the eye. "I guess I will," I mumble. "You can have everything in the house." But then my feelings catch up with me and I begin to cry. "Peggy, Peggy," I sputter, taking hold of her shoulders. "Please give me another chance. I'm so sorry for everything I've done. If you'll only give me another chance, I promise I'll change!" Tears are streaming down my face.

But Peggy stands before me like stone, saying nothing. She only stares icily into my eyes and shakes her head. There is no question now. It is over. There is nothing I can do. I destroyed her trust in me. Finally she speaks. "I think the sooner you move out, the better. You'll still be able to visit Jeff. He'll always know who his father is."

Calling my parents in Spain, I feel desperate for some sympathy. But I don't really tell them the whole story. I merely state that Peggy wants to leave me and that she's filing for a divorce. I want them to believe it's her fault. I don't mention that I had an affair or that I have had several girlfriends. Mom and Dad, to my surprise, don't jump on my case right away.

"Are you open to counseling?" Dad asks.

"Yes, I am," I lie. "I really don't want this divorce." *Anything I can say to make me look good*, I think.

"What will happen with Jeffrey?"

"Peggy will keep him, and she says I'll be able to see him whenever I want," I explain.

"Well, Jon, do what you can and we'll be praying for you," my parents tell me before hanging up. *Funny, I think as I turn from the phone, I don't feel criticized by Mom and Dad, but I don't feel much support from them either.* I later discover that Peggy has called them earlier and told them all about my lies and involvements with other women. *I guess they have reasons not to give me support at this time. I haven't been open and honest with them, either.*

As I descend to the basement to sift through my things, I ponder what it's like to become a divorce statistic. My eyes again fill with tears as I wonder how in the world I'll be able to say good-bye to Jeff. At age one, he's not old enough to understand, but very soon he'll be able to ask, "Where's Daddy?" *How does a divorced parent answer that question?* I ask myself.

As I pick through the green plastic bags of my belongings and memoirs, I can't stop thinking about Jeff. All those things I wanted for him as I watched him in the hospital nursery—they'll probably never happen now. I'll miss out on my own son's growing up.

The prospect of leaving Jeff behind embitters me toward Peggy all the more. I consider various ways to get back at her for what she's done—even suicide. *That would show her how much misery she's put me through,* I muse.

Somehow I manage to finish sorting through the bags. Then I consolidate my pickings and carry them up the basement stairs. At the top step, Jeff is standing in his walker, gazing at me in silence as if he knows something is wrong. For what seems like the twentieth time today, I am unable to hold back the tears. I pick him up and hold him tightly.

"Jeff—my little Jeff," I choke out. "I may not be around to see you grow up, but I want you to know that I will always love you and I'll never forget you as long as I live."

I go outside and walk around the block several times so I can regain my composure. *How could this have happened?* I ask over and over. *What went wrong? Isn't there anything I can do to change this?*

Unfortunately, my bitterness and self-pity prevent me from seeing why it hurts so much: my early childhood history is repeating itself. Once again I am being abandoned, just as my real parents abandoned me. Even worse, I am now continuing the pattern by abandoning my own son. But I am not ready to understand this truth yet, nor do I recognize how my indiscretions have contributed to it.

All I feel is the pain, and it cuts so deeply that I only want to block it out somehow, to run away from it. *If Peggy doesn't want me, I'll find someone else who does*, I vow. Grudgingly I resolve to get on with my life, rationalizing that it would be best for all of us. I return to the house, pack up the Bronco, and say my final good-byes. At about noon that hot Saturday, I drive off, leaving Peggy and my son behind.

Though vascillating between wanting to be around people and wanting to be alone, I have arranged to stay with Steve and Jill, a couple I work with at the hospital. After driving around aimlessly for an hour, I arrive at their house. I don't say much to them; instead, I try to keep busy by going out and washing the Bronco. Already I miss being with Peggy. Or rather, I don't miss Peggy as much as I miss *belonging* to someone. The loneliness of being abandoned pulls at me so strongly that I think I'll do nearly anything just to be with someone who cares about me.

As I wipe the watermarks from the car, a face pops into my mind: Nanci, the girl at Deb's party the other night. *She'll make me feel better—why don't I track her down?* I hop into the Bronco and stop by the hospital to get her address. Then I drive to her house, where she warmly invites me in. I stay with Nanci for the rest of that Saturday evening—and for the next few days.

Part of me senses the craziness of my actions—moving in with a woman I hardly know on the same day that I leave my wife. But over the years I have taught myself how to react to difficult situations—when the going gets tough, I move on to the next adventure. Or person. It's too hard to deal with the pain of understanding why things happen the way they do. Better to block it out and move on to something new. And this is exactly what I am doing now with Nanci.

Initially we get along well. Nanci, recently divorced herself, has a baby daughter, Kelly, who is a few months older than Jeff. She has been renting a house, and since her lease is about to end, I offer to buy a house for the three of us to live in. Within the next few weeks I locate a two-bedroom brick home only a couple of blocks from the hospital, and I proceed with the purchase. The garage badly needs a paint job, so we invite over all of our hospital nursing friends one Saturday to scrape and repaint.

I'm growing weary of the stress at the Community Hospital emergency room. Since I began working here, the pace has sped up considerably. During the evening shift alone, we now treat between 150 and 250 "ordinary" patients. In addition, we must handle the "trauma" patients—victims of stabbings, shootings, heart attacks, or serious car accidents.

But the job stress doesn't bother me nearly as much as the strained staff relationships. My co-workers and I are at odds with each other, and changing rules and policies make me more disgruntled. I decide to look for a job at another hospital.

Before long I have joined the staff of Riley Pediatric Hospital, where I still work in ER, but only with children. The position appeals to me because I have a special love for kids. I am reminded of the fun times Pele and I had playing soccer with the boys and girls in New York. And having had a child of my own gives me further desire to help these patients.

On the job, I quickly learn that pediatrics is totally different from adult medicine. The doctors use different drugs on children, and different amounts. A baby's condition can change more quickly from good to bad and vice versa. The pace seems even faster, the intensity greater. Working with adults, I was always able to show compassion, yet remain emotionally detached. With the children, however, I find myself getting much more emotionally involved. If a baby dies during the day, I go home severely depressed—almost as if my own baby has died.

One day a baby boy in critical condition arrives by helicopter, with a fractured skull, multiple lacerations on his back and arms, and bruises on his lower body. We are told the baby has suffered a fall. Before we have a chance to evaluate his precise condition, the baby goes into cardiac arrest. Frantically we work to save him with CPR and every other available method, but the heart monitor refuses to show anything but a straight line. The doctor finally says, "That's it—stop."

We all stand silently and look at the dead child. For

an eternal moment, I hope that a miracle will happen and the baby will revive. Nothing. My mind wanders to my own son, about the same age as this little boy. What if Jeff had just died in front of me? What would I do? A great sorrow grips me.

Later I discover the true cause of the baby's injuries. He had been learning to walk and, while the parents were present, had jostled the table and spilled the father's coffee. In a fit of rage, the father jumped up and beat the child—to death, as it turned out. What's worse, however, is that the parents show no remorse for their act of murder. No charges are filed against them, and the official autopsy report makes no mention of the child being beaten. The injustice of it all leads me to think about leaving pediatrics altogether—perhaps even the whole medical career I have been pursuing.

I stop by my old house—now Peggy's—to visit Jeffrey. I want to see him so much, but every time I do, Peggy complains to me about something. She tells me I don't give her enough money, or that the car I left her doesn't run well and I should fix it, or that I came at a bad time.

We end up arguing right in front of Jeffrey, which only makes me feel worse. On top of that, when I need to leave, Jeff screams and hangs on to me and tells me to stay. By the time I get back to my car, I'm an emotional basket case.

Wondering what to do about my relationship with Nanci is an ongoing issue. We have gotten our blood tests and our marriage license, but we somehow don't find the time or motivation to actually get married. In the meantime, Nanci seems to be developing cabin fever and wants to be out on her own. On several occasions, while I stay home and take care of Kelly, I learn that Nanci is out with other guys. I am furious.

So how do I deal with it? The same way I've always handled problem situations: I turn my back, assume it's someone else's fault, and move on. I figure that Indianapolis isn't big enough for me, an ex-wife, and an ex-lover. Though I'm completely fed up with life in this city, I play the gentleman, the nice guy who will make life easier for everyone else by leaving. So I decide to pick up and go south, to a state that I hear has lots of work and lots of excitement: Texas.

This departure carries none of the excruciating agony of my last one. I know I will miss Jeffrey, but I also feel a mixture of excitement and fear about venturing out into the unknown. On my final day in Indiana, I pack everything I can fit into the Bronco: my clothes, my trophies, my weights and bench. A new color TV I have just bought won't fit, so I leave it with Nanci. Late that Monday evening, I take off for Houston with $150 in my pocket. The sky is dark and clear.

Nine

Deceptive Escapism

Daydreaming about what Texas will be like as I
drive, hour after hour. I have many stereotyped
notions of what to expect, and as I approach the
state line, I reflect on how many of them
might be true.

*D*o most of the people really drive Cadillacs? And do the rest either drive trucks or ride horses? Is everything really bigger in Texas? Does everyone brag about being best or biggest? Does everyone wear cowboy hats?

I also wonder what I want to do here. There is an economic boom in Texas and I plan to quickly land a decent job and make some good money. After that, who knows? *Maybe I'll meet a good-looking Southern girl, get married, and live happily ever after. We'll buy ourselves a nice house, maybe have a couple of kids. . . .*

My thoughts are blasted away by the air horn of a tractor-trailer behind me. My Bronco has wandered into his lane.

Finally arriving in Texas via Interstate 30. I drive through Texarkana and several other small towns until I see signs for Houston. Then I turn south. To my disappointment, the state looks just like the others I have endured for the past eighteen hours. I see a few Caddys, a few pickups, and a few farms, but very little that confirms my stereotyped images—except the enormous size of the state. I assumed that once I crossed the state line, I'd be almost to Houston, but now I discover it's another five hours away.

When I eventually get to Houston, I have only forty dollars left. I cruise to the south side of town and locate a cheap motel to stay in. To my surprise, when I walk into the motel lobby, I find all sorts of people who, like me, have just come to Houston to seek their fortunes. I talk to a guy with a single room who lets me sleep on his floor and split the room cost. Pleased with my progress so far, I determine to go right out in the morning and find a job.

Noticing a racquetball club two blocks from the motel, I figure I shouldn't have too much trouble getting work there, since I have stayed in good shape. I walk in and apply. To my amazement, they hire me the same day and ask me to start immediately. For the next few weeks, I work days at the club and continue to stay at the motel.

Then I am asked to serve as the evening manager and sleep on the premises, since the club has been broken into on several occasions. I leap at the opportunity, because now I won't have to pay for the motel. I am my own boss, and I am free to invite friends (specifically, girls) to join me in the hot tub after hours. And, if this isn't enough, I still have my days free. What job could be better?

I take full advantage of my benefits. Over the next six months, I make plenty of money, stay in shape, and meet lots of girls. But business at the racquetball club slows down, and eventually I opt for a position as bouncer for a rapidly growing nightclub.

One of the girls I date for a few weeks asks me to move into her apartment with her. After three or four months of living together, however, I realize she wants to settle down and I am not yet ready for that. So I look for another roommate. A big guy named Jim frequents the bar, and I find out he has a dependable job with an oil company and needs a roommate himself. We decide to get a place together.

I marvel at what a wild and crazy guy Jim is! He is 6'2", 200 pounds, and nearly unbeatable at shooting pool. He also loves racquetball, so between the bar, the racquetball club, and the house we rent, we spend lots of time together and become good friends.

Like me, Jim is outgoing and loves to party. And also like me, Jim loves to drink. But he gets carried away with it more often than I do. On a typical weekend night, he knocks off five, six, or seven beers, then tries to pick up girl after girl until he can convince one of them to spend the night with him. Sometimes he lands a "straight" girl; other times he ends up with a hooker. Though in some ways I'm as wild as Jim, I still view him as having gone further "over the edge" than I have. Yet we get along well and enjoy living together for the next year.

One day at home I hear Jim come in and disappear

into his room. He has been acting more aloof lately, and for the past few weeks I've hardly seen him at the club at all. I knock on his door and ask if we can talk. He is sitting on the side of his bed, looking at the floor.

"Jim," I say, "what's been going on? Where have you been? I haven't seen you at the club lately—is everything okay?"

He looks up at me, and tears fill his eyes. *What could be the matter?* I wonder. *Jim is such an easygoing, yet strong sort of guy. What could have gone wrong for him?*

Finally he speaks. "Jon—I just found out I have herpes." At these words, he puts his head in his hands and sobs. I stand there looking at him, not knowing what to say. Inside, a self-righteous part of me wants to say, "Hey, what do you expect when you fool around the way you do?" But I remain silent.

Later I give myself a little pep talk. *I never need to worry about getting into predicaments like Jim,* I muse. First of all, the girls are crazy about me. I never have to chase after them like Jim does—they come to me. I don't have to settle for hookers and their diseases. *Besides,* I tell myself, *I am invincible.* Things like that just don't happen to me. I beat the odds all through high school and college and professional soccer. I picked myself up after getting burned in Indianapolis, and in a year and a half I have carved out a good life here in Houston. I make loads of money, drive my own Mazda RX-7, and have just been promoted to manager of one of the largest nightclubs in the city. My conclusion: *I don't have to worry about getting in trouble.*

Soon I try cocaine for the first time. I have just finished my check-outs and closed up the bar after a record cash intake for a Friday night. I decide to meet a few of the other managers and bartenders afterward to play cards and unwind. At about four in the morning, we are sitting around the coffee table, talking "shop" and having a few drinks. The radio blasts from across the room.

Then one of the guys stands up and reaches into his pocket. "Guess who stopped by my bar tonight?" he says with a smirk. He pulls out a small plastic baggie containing a white powdery substance, and carefully pours about half of it on the table.

My eyes widen. Being in the nightclub business, I hear the staff talk about coke all the time, but this is the first time I've seen it up close. I quickly realize that everyone here except me has tried it before; they're eager to get their hit. The guy then goes into his wallet for a razor blade and can't find one, so he removes his driver's license instead. As I watch him divide up the powder into equal amounts with his license, I know I have a choice to make.

Silently I argue with myself: *Keep yourself clean, Jon. Stay away from this stuff—it's dangerous.* But the other side of me chimes in: *Oh, don't worry, just trying it once won't hurt you—you'll be all right. No one except these guys will know. Now's as good a time as any to find out what it's like. You won't get hooked just using it once. Look at these other guys here. They don't look like druggies, do they? Besides, if you're the only one who doesn't try it, they might stop liking you, or call you a "narc," or ask you to leave. You don't want that, do you?*

Another guy stands and removes a crisp new hundred-dollar bill from his wallet. He rolls it up tight, like a short straw, and leans over his portion of coke, which he has divided in half. With the rolled-up bill, he snorts half into one nostril, and half into the other. Then he sits back and smiles. There is a gleam in his eyes, as if he has just been hit with the greatest sensation in the world. He passes the bill to the next person.

As I watch, I wonder: *Look at how good he feels—it's so obvious! And the feeling hits instantly! How can anything that makes you feel that good be bad for you?* After several guys indulge, I hear them talking in "coke language," saying things like, "Who brought the blow?" or "That was a good line" or "There are even some rocks in that gram." I listen carefully, because I don't want to appear ignorant about the terminology.

My turn comes last. The server, still using the license, scrapes all the coke remains on the table into one final "line"—by far the largest portion of the evening. The rolled-up bill is passed to me. I have no idea what the normal "dosage" is, and I worry momentarily whether I can handle it. *What happens if I have a heart attack? Maybe I should act like a nice guy and offer to share the line with someone so they won't know I'm scared.*

Then one of the guys says, "Hey, Jon—bet you can't take in that whole line in one snort!"

That is all I need to hear. I take one look at him, then lean over the table. Catching a glimpse of myself in the glass tabletop, I am frightened for a split second at what I am about to do. But I won't stop now. I focus on the big line of coke, bring my nose down to the rolled-up bill, and snort up the entire line into one nostril.

Wow! I am rocked by the most powerful, most wonderful feeling I have ever experienced—even better than sex. Every phrase I could use to describe it falls short. I feel like a million bucks. I feel cool. I feel tough. On top of the world. Like I can do anything. More invincible than ever.

And if this isn't enough, the guys around me are cheering my performance. I have strengthened their respect for me by doing this; they like me even more now.

Sitting back in my chair, I congratulate myself for what I have done. *How can anyone not want this experience?* I muse. *This is what every guy needs. If I have a bad night, I can use this and I'll feel better. Even on a good night, this stuff will make it even better. And now I can easily make friends or get girls simply by offering them some "blow."*

My first hit thrills me so much that only an hour later I walk out to one of my friends, money in hand, looking for someone I can buy more coke from. A bartender friend directs me to a "trustworthy" source—a guy named Don—and from that day he becomes my cocaine supplier.

I weigh up small bags of coke with Don in an undisclosed apartment. By the time we finish I am so high I can hardly read the numbers on the scale. Yet somehow I don't feel as high as that first time. I want to snort even more, but I worry about overdosing.

At first I limit myself to half a gram of cocaine per night, but soon I am using a lot more—sometimes as much as three or four grams on a big night. It seems there are so many excellent opportunities to use coke—at parties, to meet girls, after a "bad day."

My habit grows to the point that I have to watch my budget. At $100 a gram, I find myself forking out between $500 and $700 each week for the stuff. With my good salary and the bar business booming, I can afford it right now, but not indefinitely. I try to figure out how to maintain my steady coke supply without going broke.

Ten

Flirting with Death

Thinking that I have my cocaine habit under control, when actually I don't. To pay for my own supply, I begin to sell coke to some of my close friends.

I nstead of pocketing the money, I go right out and buy larger quantities of coke for myself, thereby snorting up all my profits. Before long my situation mushrooms. The more coke I need—for myself or for parties—the more I must sell. And the more money I make, the more I want to make. Eventually the quantities and the deals get so big and serious that it scares me. But I always proceed anyway, assuming it'll all work out somehow.

One day my friend Tim and I prepare to depart for Miami, where we are supposed to complete a major deal with some Panamanians. Everything has been set up for us. Friday evening we arrive in Miami with $80,000 cash, and we make sure we have our game plan straight. The deal is scheduled to go down Saturday night.

Our arrangements sound like an episode of "Miami Vice." We are supposed to wait in our car near a predetermined alley and, when the dealer shows up, are to give a code word to indicate we are the proper buyers and not cops. We decide to split the money into two portions. Tim will get into the man's car and give him half the cash. When he is sure the dealer has the full amount of cocaine, he will give me a signal, and I will come over with the rest of the money and complete the deal.

Though we have both carried out transactions like this before, we are more afraid than usual this time because we are dealing with Panamanians. They are reputedly the most brutal of all drug dealers, possessing no respect for human life (their own included) or for a "straight" business deal. They all carry guns and don't hesitate to use them. Many of them are strung out on drugs even as they're doing business, and they have little patience for anything that doesn't go exactly their way. All they care about is getting their money.

On Saturday, we lie around at the motel most of the day. At about four in the afternoon, we decide to stop in at a little bar and have a few drinks to "prepare" for our evening escapade. There we meet a couple of girls and drink with them for a while. *Oh, how I wish we had some "snow,"* I say to myself.

As it begins to get dark outside, we know it's nearly time to carry out our deal. We tell the girls to wait for us, that we'll be back in an hour or so with a surprise for them. We head off in our rental car to find the appointed meeting place. I am quite nervous.

We find the spot, then wait until something happens. Tim turns to me and says, "Okay, do we have it straight? I go in, you hold your money at the top of the alley, and I call you when I'm ready. Got it?"

Only a moment later, a white Porsche Carrera pulls up. The tinted window glides down, and a dark face stares at us. I repeat the code word. He tells us to follow him. For the next ten minutes I chase him up and down the Miami streets as he tries to make sure no one is following us. Then he brings his car to a halt.

As I edge my car alongside his, the window again lowers. "Who's coming with me?" he says. Tim glares at him, then slowly gets out of my car and moves toward the Porsche, carrying nothing but a concealed paper bag with $40,000 in it. He barely gets himself into the car when the tires squeal and the car takes off. Worried about my partner, I floor the accelerator and follow once again. In and out of the night traffic we weave, until finally he slows down and turns into a narrow alley. I ease up to the curb and wait, positioned so I can see his car clearly.

It is a quiet evening; a half-moon glows in the clear sky. I check my watch and wait for a sign from Tim. I don't know exactly what the sign will be, but I know I'll recognize it. These deals always take a little while to complete. Fifteen minutes pass—usually the maximum time needed. I begin to worry. Twenty minutes. Still no sign.

I am nearly in a state of panic when I see the passenger door open a crack. Sighing with relief, I now know the sign will come through any minute and then we can get out of here. Already I picture picking up the girls, going back to our hotel room and enjoying this new coke shipment. I smile at the anticipated pleasure.

Suddenly, two gunshots pierce the night. They are

from the Porsche. Something has gone wrong. My eyes riveted to the passenger door, I quickly reach for my own .357 Smith & Wesson, which I keep on hand for "emergencies." My heart is racing. A second later, the door flies open and Tim rolls out onto the pavement. The Porsche squeals down the alley and disappears. Tim doesn't move.

I am frozen with fear. *Now what do I do?* I fret. *Should I drive up and see if Tim is still alive? Should I just leave him there and hope someone will find him and help him? But what if the police come? Even worse, what if the Panamanians come back to get me?* I decide that I can't just leave Tim, so I slowly pull into the alley with only my parking lights on. I look around to make sure I haven't been seen; then I get out and tiptoe over to Tim, who lies face up and still. I am now dripping with sweat.

"Tim, can you hear me?" I whisper, hoping that he will at least move a little. *No response!*

I grab his shoulder to turn him over and check for wounds. His body is stiff, and when I move him, I see two bullet holes in the back of his neck. From my medical experience I can tell immediately that he is dead.

The next moment seems to last an eternity. As I stand there, soaked in sweat, next to Tim's lifeless body, an image comes to mind. I picture Tim standing before God, trying to give some account of his life. Then a question strikes me: *What if I had been killed instead of Tim? What would I say to God?*

My heart pounds as I consider—for a split second—the crummy way I've lived much of my life. But the prospect of facing God scares me so much that I quickly turn my attention to the tragedy at hand. *Tim is dead, and on top of it, I've just lost $40,000. Since I'm a witness to the murder, the Panamanians might* *come after me next.* Terror-stricken and wondering how I'll ever escape from this nightmare, I jump in my car and, leaving Tim behind, rush back to my motel.

I lock myself in my room, worrying that I'm being watched. Several hours later, the waiting gets to me and I decide to venture out for something to eat. I drive to an area of Miami that I know well and look for a restaurant. But I am so nervous and upset that I can the dinner idea at the last minute and buy some "blow" on the street. I go back to my room and get myself higher than a kite.

Unfortunately, even $300 of coke doesn't make Tim come back to life or return the $40,000 to me. Nor can I shake those nagging thoughts about how narrowly *I* missed having to face eternity. After coming down a little, I go to a pay phone and reserve a plane flight home that night. I drop off the car and take a cab to the airport.

The cocaine heightens my paranoia as I wait to board my flight. I still worry that a band of dred-locked Panamanians will show up in the terminal with sawed-off shotguns and blow me away. To calm my nerves, I drag myself over to a bar and pour down several cocktails. Before long I am such a drunken mess that I almost miss my flight.

On the plane, I keep thinking about Tim. *Will anyone show up to claim his body? Did anyone see me with him? What will his family think when they find out? What if I had been in Tim's place? Would he have driven off and left me behind? Maybe I should have at least buried him somewhere. But maybe I'd have gotten caught, too.* And then again I see that horrifying image of Tim and me, standing before God. The more I think about what happened, the more I sweat and the more I drink.

My other partner, Don, is waiting for me as I stumble through the terminal gate in Houston. In badly slurred speech I attempt to explain what happened, and he stands there, stunned. On the way home, Don tells me we have to come up with a new game plan to replace the lost money, which another man had put up for the deal. We are so deep into trouble that we ignore the fact that Tim has died and worry about money instead.

We decide not to tell the man what happened, and instead plan to sell more cocaine to make up the lost money. Then we'll return it to him. *Sure we will*, I think. He thinks otherwise, though, and hires a hit man to kill us.

Eleven

Living on the Edge

*Considering the idea of getting out of drug deal-
ing. My friend Tim has died because of it. And I
now have to replace $40,000
of someone else's money.*

I'm not too worried about replacing the money. I
can make that up with no sweat. But when I
hear that someone is out to dispose of me
because the deal went sour, I fear for my life. I don't like
these mega-drug deals with all their weapons and secre-
cy. Depression strikes me frequently. I wonder what I've
gotten myself into, and if I can ever get myself out.
What will it take? Apparently more than I've experienced so far!

Rather than take a hard look at my situation, I simply pull out a few lines of cocaine whenever I get

depressed. In a matter of moments my old feeling of strength and power returns, and I tell myself, *Look, Jon, the bar business is booming and the drug business is flourishing. Why get out now?* So I keep working with Don, and together we keep going after bigger and bigger purchases of cocaine.

As our drug business grows, we find ourselves working with a higher echelon of drug wholesalers. Rarely, if ever, do we need to fool around with the crazy Panamanians anymore. And a higher level of dealers leads to a higher level of clients, which in turn brings in more money.

At one point Don and I fly to Columbia, where we set up a few contacts and pick up several major shipments of coke. This time everything goes as planned; we return safely to the States and deliver our goods up and down the East Coast. We take in more money than we know what to do with—several hundred thousand dollars.

Another time we bring in so much coke that I temporarily store it in the frame of my king-sized waterbed. It completely fills the space, so I am unable to put the water mattress back on. I stand back and think, *Whew—at $100 a gram, that's a heck of a lot of cocaine.* I throw a few sheets over the stuff and sleep on it that night, as if I am guarding the First National Bank.

I discover it's possible to go for a week at a time without sleep. Cocaine causes the body to produce mass quantities of adrenaline, which makes you feel hyper-awake and hyper-alert. In short, you go sky-high. It feels so good that you want more and more coke so you don't have to "come down." At the same time, of course, coke—which is a depressant—numbs your nervous system and can cause your body to shut down completely if you take enough. But we don't worry. We have so much of it around us that we stay high around the clock and sponsor wild parties—virtual orgies—that last for days.

There is no deeper level of debauchery than what we stoop to at these parties. "Straight" girls or hookers—we don't care. If they ask for money, we pay them with all the coke they want. In exchange, they perform every imaginable perverse sexual act—with each other, with us, with a whole group of people. After a seven-, eight-, or ten-day cocaine binge, combined with several extended parties, I drop into bed and sleep for nearly four days. But when I awaken, I feel empty, lonely, and sad.

At this point in my life, however, I have such a whacked-out view of the world that I assume partying and being high are normal. If I wake up miserable every now and then, it only means I need a few more lines and a few more girls. The emptiness never seems to go away, though.

Holidays only intensify the loneliness—especially Christmas. It should be such a happy time, because families unite and celebrate together, and because it's the time we marvel at how God sent his son Jesus to earth. I still remember what my parents taught me about Christmas, and I think I still believe it. But the holiday still depresses me, because everyone else seems to have family they can go to. I have cut myself off from my parents and relatives, and I usually spend Christmas alone. I watch a church service on TV, then turn off the set and hit the coke real heavy that day.

When I reevaluate my drug involvement from time to time, I wonder whether I should get out. I see people's lives, including my own, being messed up. I've seen my friend die. But I can't "just say no" and quit. It's not that easy. First of all, if I immediately stop buying and selling, my "business associates" will automatically be suspicious of me. They'll think the police picked me up and that I'll turn them in. My personal safety may be jeopardized. Certainly my income will drop dramatically, and my lifestyle will have to change.

Second, all my friends are into drugs; getting out will mean losing them. *If that happens,* I consider, *what kind of friends are they anyhow?* But they're all I have—and as far back as I can remember I have needed the affirmation and approval of friends to make me feel okay. Amazingly, this need has almost more power over me than the cocaine itself. The prospect of losing my friends towers over such other potential losses as money and coke. So I stay in, despite having to witness more painful and sometimes very frightening situations.

Once, with some friends, I try a drug known as Ecstasy for the first time. Ecstasy is a hallucinogen mixed with testosterone, a steroid that has unpredictable side effects. Since my friends have all just taken it and seem to be having a good time, I figure it'll be all right for me.

Wrong! It has anything but an "ecstatic" effect on me. Instead, the drug gives me a sense of hard, cold reality—the very *last* thing I want it to do. Coke is my big escape from pain and stress and pressure; this new drug is doing just the opposite. For a few incredibly depressing moments, I see clearly what my life has amounted to thus far: nothing. I picture my parents, heartbroken that their talented son is dealing drugs and working at a bar. And I think about God, knowing that he cannot be happy with the life I am living. I realize that this new drug-induced sense of reality is true, but I am not yet ready to face it. Quickly I dig out my stash of coke and snort away.

A guy named Ed stops over at our apartment to buy a gram. He is a regular, reliable customer and always pays cash. As soon as he makes his purchase, however, he usually sits right down and injects the coke directly into his veins, which is more dangerous than snorting (and more gross to watch). Don and I usually ask him to shoot up in the bathroom.

Occasionally Ed visits in a very messed-up state because he has bought his coke from someone else and gotten a bad batch. Our stuff is very pure and gives a "clean" high, so we take care of him by giving him a fresh dose. We like Ed, but worry about him as his desperation visits grow more frequent.

One night Don and I decide to go to bed early—at about 3:00 A.M. Just as I'm about to doze off, I hear a knock at the door, but not just a regular knock. I sense it's the kind of knock that means trouble. I reach under my other pillow, pull out my .357 police special, and quickly make sure it is loaded. Then I tiptoe to Don's room and tell him we have company.

Another knock comes from the door, along with some kind of shuffling outside. Don grabs his .38 and we slowly approach the door. Silently I look through the peep hole, but see nothing since the hall light is burned out. "Who's there?" Don shouts in his South American accent. "Who are you and what do you want?" We raise our guns.

Silence.

Then from the bottom of the door, we hear a weak, nearly weeping voice: "It's me—Ed. Please let me in. I'm in a real bad way—I need some stuff to straighten me out." We remain quiet, listening to see if anyone else is in the hall.

"C'mon, guys, I'm really hurting," Ed sputters. "Let me in, please. I need help bad." We realize that if we don't let him in, Ed may make a scene in the hall and attract attention. So I slowly open the door.

Ed crumples onto our floor. Quickly I grab his arm and drag him inside. One look at him makes me gasp. His eyes are bloodshot and bulging out of their sockets. His skin is ashen, cold, and clammy, almost like the corpses I saw when I worked at the hospital. His veins are collapsed, and needle marks run up and down both of his arms. It seems as though half the blood has been drained from his body. I can hardly bear to touch him.

Don and I look at him lying on the floor, then look at each other, wondering what to do. *This is so unreal,* I think. *How can someone get himself into this situation? He's practically dead—yet he's coming to us for more cocaine!*

Ed turns his gray, sweaty face toward us and barely mumbles the words we are afraid to hear: "Guys, I need help—fix me a shot. If I don't get one I think I'll die." He struggles to point to his back pocket, where he carries all his drug paraphernalia.

Since Don has done most of the dealing with Ed, I decide to step back and let him handle this. Don again looks at me with fear and despair in his eyes. We both know that if Ed ingests any more snow, he'll surely die. And we don't want any part of that. But Ed continues to beg and plead with us as he lies on the floor, and we realize that if we don't give him some coke soon, he'll go into withdrawal seizures and die right here on our floor anyway.

We sit in silence for a long time, interrupted only by an occasional twitch from Ed. Finally Don reaches for

Ed's back pocket to remove his paraphernalia. Instantly a smile of satisfaction comes over Ed's face. I can hardly believe what I am seeing—a man nearly dead who wants yet one more shot, even if he has to die for it. Don fixes the shot; after jabbing Ed's collapsed veins numerous times, he finally gets the needle in.

Almost immediately Ed goes into a seizure and begins to flop around on the floor. As a trained nurse, I know exactly what to do in this situation; and the very worst thing one can do is inject someone with a substance such as cocaine. Yet, instead of grabbing Don's hand and yanking out the needle, I drop to the floor and hold Ed down. My muscles know they should be moving differently, but they freeze in position around Ed as I watch Don continue to shoot him up. Finally he finishes, and we hold Ed in place for a few extremely long minutes until the seizure subsides.

I look at Ed, lying there motionless, and suddenly see Tim's face. Miami, the Panamanian dealer with the Porsche, the gunshots, and worst of all, Tim's dead body in the alley—all flash through my head. *Here I am again, standing over a virtually dead body. What am I going to do this time? What happens if he dies? How will we explain what happened? Or how will we dispose of the body? What if we get caught?*

We sit and wait for a few minutes to see if Ed regains consciousness. Some coke users pass out briefly after a fix, and we hope that Ed comes out of it shortly. Ten minutes go by. Ed still hasn't moved. When I check him, his pulse and breathing are barely discernible; his body is getting colder. Now our concern and fear turns to terror. We talk back and forth, trying to justify ourselves and figure out what to do. "We weren't trying to kill him," Don says defensively. "We were only trying to help the poor guy."

"Yet how can we explain this to anyone?" I respond. "And who will believe our story if we do? How can this be happening to us?"

By now it is after 4:00 A.M. and still dark. We decide to carry Ed outside and leave him somewhere. Our twisted logic is that if he stays alive, someone will find him and help; if he dies, no one will be able to blame us. We make the decision, but for some reason neither of us can bring himself to attempt to move Ed.

I badly want to deny what is happening, to block it out. I am actually participating in another person's death. I can't face it, or face myself. And I can tell Don feels the same way. So once again I deal with reality by trading it for non-reality: I go into my room, to my private stash, and take out a white rock of the purest cocaine, slightly smaller than my palm. It sparkles with a faint yellow glow, and I can almost hear it calling out to me. "Here I am—exactly what you need," I think it is saying. "Once you have me, you won't need anything else. With me, you can go to Never-Worry Land and forget all your troubles."

A man is dying on my living room floor from cocaine, and our solution is to snort ourselves silly. Don and I cut up the rock and smooth it down into powder. For the next couple of hours we proceed to snort up every trace of it, getting higher and higher and yet still wanting more. So we break out more of our stash and pour the powder into cigarettes. What a powerful rush! And still I want another and another. I take such big hits that my heart feels like it will jump out of my chest. Sometimes the rush is so strong that I fall back in my chair.

Before the morning dawns, Don and I muster the courage to take Ed outside and leave him a few miles away. When we later hear that he has died from a drug overdose, we act surprised. But we ask no questions.

Moving on to yet another adventure is my way of trying to forget the pain I heap on myself. Cocaine is my perennial escape—from a bad day, from a broken heart, from my own mistakes, from a painful past. My favorite thing to do is sit back with my headphones on, crank up the rock 'n' roll, and snort my brains out. That way I don't have to think about anything. I can just feel good.

I meet a new friend, Tom, who likes to "freebase" his cocaine. First he heats it over the stove until it turns to a yellow sticky paste. Then he spreads the paste on a plate and lets it sit for a few moments until it hardens. Finally he scrapes the hardened substance off and places it in a glass pipe, which we take turns smoking. Prepared this way, the coke gives a more potent, more addictive high than snorting.

Because of our common interest in cocaine, Tom and I spend a lot of time together over the next year. Between ourselves and the girls we party with, we sometimes go through two or three thousand dollars' worth of blow in one sitting. I am finding that no matter how often I get high or how much cocaine I use, it never seems to satisfy enough. So we constantly seek new ways to get a better buzz—by taking bigger hits, cooking the stuff differently, or mixing it with other drugs.

Yet the void in me continues to grow. I have now been living "on the edge" for several years, and I wonder how much longer I'll be able to hold on before I slip off.

Twelve

Time to Take Stock?

Transferring to a newly opened bar in Dallas. I
don't have a great deal of choice in the matter. I
am told by the corporation's new vice president
that if I don't take the position of manager of Cafe
Dallas, I am out of a job.

I agree to make the move. A few friends help me
pack up a U-Haul truck and drive it north to
Dallas, while I follow in my car. We all stop for
gas along the way, and I take two big hits of blow.
Shortly after we get back on the road, a state trooper
appears out of nowhere and begins to tail me.

His presence unnerves me, not only because I am
high and need to "sober up," but also because I am carrying a quarter-ounce of coke in the car, under the passenger seat. Just as I start to wonder where to hide it if

the trooper pulls me over, I see his flashing lights in my rear-view mirror. *Oh, great!* I groan silently.

At first I am frantic, inside and out. I squirm and shift in my seat, then reach under the passenger seat for the small cocaine packet. Fortunately, the tinted glass on my rear window prevents the cop from seeing how restless I am. Fear and coke combine to send my thoughts racing: *Where do I hide it? What if he finds it? Is he allowed to search my car? Why is he pulling me over anyway?* As I coast onto the shoulder and slow down, I look into the mirror and try to calm myself. I wonder how I look—whether my eyes are bloodshot and whether there is any telltale powder around my nose. The troopers—I see two of them—are getting out of the car and coming toward me. Quickly I stuff the coke into my shorts and hope for the best.

One officer approaches from my side of the car, the other from the passenger side. As they both peer cautiously into my open windows, the trooper on my side suddenly shouts, "Concealed weapon!" and reaches for his gun. Shocked, I quickly turn and see that my .357 is lying on the other seat in plain sight. It must have slipped out of its cover.

"Don't worry, officer—it's not loaded," I announce, sweating profusely. His hand still on his gun, the trooper asks me to step out of the car. He is a tall man, and I can tell he is quite edgy. I am extremely nervous myself and dread thinking about what will happen next.

In a brisk, authoritative tone, he says, "I think you need to come over to the police car and explain why you are carrying that weapon." I concentrate on walking smoothly and straight, aware that they're watching to see if I'm under the influence of anything. Meanwhile, the other cop begins to search my car lightly, under the seats and in back.

As we sit in the police car, the first officer pelts me with questions: "What do you do for a living? What kind of work are you involved in? Why are you carrying a gun?"

By now I have had a moment to collect my thoughts and get my story straight. I tell him I am the manager of a nightclub, and that I am in the process of moving my belongings to Dallas, where I have been transferred. I have a gun, I explain, because in my job I carry large sums of money to the bank each day and have been advised to keep a gun with me. The story is basically true, though, of course, I don't divulge the *main* reason I carry the gun.

I think he believes me. He pauses for a moment, then picks up his radio mike and calls in my license number for a check. "I'm going to be issuing you a citation for a burnt-out tail-light bulb," he says.

My heart beats so loudly that I worry whether the officer can hear it. As we sit there waiting, the radio buzzes and squawks with various names, addresses, numbers, and police codes. Then the trooper abruptly turns to me and asks, "Have you been drinking or doing any kind of drugs?"

The question throws me for a loop. *Does he know something I don't? Do I look that obvious?* I am sure the shock registers on my face. Quickly I recover and use the shock to my advantage. "No, sir," I respond, trying to sound self-righteous. "I haven't been doing *any* of those things. I just want to get to my new home and get there safely." Apparently my answer satisfies him, because he makes no further mention of the subject.

Finally my name blares over the radio, followed by six words that are music to my ears: "No wants and no warrants—clear." I relax, but not too much. The cop agrees to dismiss my ticket and tells me I can go.

Fortunately, the packet of coke in my pants doesn't shift or fall out as I go back to my car and carefully pull away. The trooper follows me for several miles, and I stick exactly to the speed limit until he finally turns off. Only now do I let myself sigh in relief. My shirt is nearly soaked in sweat.

I take the first exit after the cop leaves and head straight for a gas station. Inside the men's room I take two major hits of coke in each nostril—so major that I nearly fall to my knees from the rush. But, oh, what a feeling!

Arriving in Dallas an hour later than the U-Haul, I casually explain to my friends that I'm late because of a routine traffic stop for a burned-out bulb. But inside I am emotionally wasted. I go straight to the new club and tell myself I need a drink or two "to wash away the road dust from the trip."

The next thing I know, it is morning, I am in a strange bed, and I have a headache. I roll over, only to find a girl sleeping next to me. I don't even know who she is. She stirs and opens her eyes.

"Where am I? What am I doing here? Who are you?" I ask, sitting up and rubbing my eyes.

"I'm Judy—one of the bartenders at Cafe Dallas," she answers. "We talked last night and I invited you over and you said yes. And here you are." She smiles. I have no memory whatsoever of the previous evening or night. When I get up, I realize that about $800 worth of cocaine I had when I first went to the club has disappeared.

I move in with Ken, who I am told is one of the company's best disc jockeys. He lives in a nice duplex in a decent area of town, so I look forward to rooming with him. At first we don't see much of each other, since I work days in the office and he DJs the evening club hours. But as we spend some late-night time together, I get to know him better—with mixed results.

Ken previously worked as DJ for a topless bar in Dallas and knows most of the dancers, so we hang out there frequently. These girls stop by our place at all hours of the night, and I love it. Something about not knowing who I might wake up with in the morning actually gives me a thrill. But even as I tell myself how exciting my life is, I realize more and more that my sexual promiscuity brings me shallow and fleeting pleasure at best. The thrill vanishes almost as fast as it comes, and I am left feeling empty.

I also learn that although Ken is the company's highest-paid DJ, he spends his money a lot faster than he makes it. Every other day he asks to borrow money from me, promising to pay me back "on Friday." But Friday never seems to come. This leads to squabbles between us, which we usually manage to patch up somehow.

We tangle on other occasions, too, such as on nights when I go to bed early and he arrives home roaring drunk. Often he shouts nonsensically, bumps into things and falls down, jerking me awake. The morning after, I get up and find him flat on his face in the doorway, asleep. Begrudgingly, I nudge him with my foot; he picks himself up and staggers into his bedroom.

The drug deals get bigger and bigger as I establish new connections and clients in Dallas. One man, a prominent banker, invites me to his luxurious estate to discuss a major coke transaction—the largest I have ever conducted. He is expecting a shipment of forty kilos of cocaine, with an estimated street value of 1.5

million dollars. It will be smuggled in a large barrel of coffee.

My mission, should I decide to accept it, is to go to Houston, make sure the coke arrives, and supervise the deal. I would receive one kilo of the shipment as payment, plus all the coke I can ingest in one sitting. I am high as he makes his proposition, and in my euphoria I tell him, "Sure, no problem."

Two weeks later I receive an anonymous call, telling me to drive a rental car to Houston, check into a certain hotel, and wait in my room for further instructions. Sure enough, once I arrive at the hotel, the phone rings again with the final details. I am scared, but the next morning I drive over to the Houston Ship Channel, wait for the proper sign, and proceed with the transaction. Everything goes as scheduled, and soon I board a pre-paid plane flight back to Dallas.

We celebrate our success the next night in plush extravagance. The banker has reserved a full-floor suite in a swanky hotel, complete with every imaginable first-class service. He arrives fashionably late with an entourage of bodyguards and foxy women. For the next forty-eight hours we smoke and snort our brains out and pursue all kinds of sexual indulgence. When the party dies down, we have consumed nearly $20,000-worth of cocaine.

Just when I think it's time to go home, the banker's helicopter picks us up at the hotel and drops us aboard his fifty-foot yacht on a nearby lake. And the party continues for another day, until I use up nearly all of my one-kilo payment of snow. I definitely plan to continue my relationship with this client.

I'm rolling with the ups and downs of the bar business. At first, things are slow since the club is so new, but in time the pace picks up and I begin to receive bonuses. Just as everything begins to look good in my career, I receive a call from one of my bar friends in Houston.

There has been a shakeup in the corporation's upper management, he tells me. People are getting fired, including one of the other vice presidents—a close friend who makes $100,000 a year and has taught me most of what I know about the bar business. I also learn that others I worked with in Houston have been let go, too. Further, Bill and Curt, the owners, are on their way to Dallas to "clean house" here as well.

Sure enough, my home phone rings early the next morning, and I am told to meet Bill and Curt at the office at 9:00 A.M. Already angered by yesterday's firing of my friends, I am ready to quit myself if they give me any trouble.

They do. . . . They tell me they are revoking all promises of salary increases made by the former management. They also say they are fed up with all the reports of cocaine abuse by the staff. I am ordered to immediately fire any staff who are known coke users.

Their harsh style ticks me off, partly because I have worked very hard for this company during the past few years and have played a major role in helping these owners become millionaires. Now I feel they're turning on me. But I am also angry because I can't risk discovery as a coke dealer. So, right there before the owners, I drop my keys on the desk and say, "Well, if that's the way you're going to operate, it sounds like you don't need me any more. Good-bye." I turn and walk out the door, planning never to return.

So mad am I that I get right into my car and drive to Houston, bringing only a few clothes with me. For the next several months, I stay there with Jack, one of the fired company executives, and we commiserate together. I sell some coke to make a little money, but Jack and I also consume a lot of it. Since I am unemployed, I have hardly any cash to buy more coke. During this time I date a very young—barely out of high school—cocktail waitress named Susan but she breaks my heart by going back to her old boyfriend.

Again I evaluate what I'm doing with my life: the bar business and the drugs. I feel a tug in me to get out of both, since neither seems to have any future. Yet, as I think of all the benefits—money, girls, excitement, and plenty of coke—I just can't bring myself to let go of my fast lifestyle. Despite the emptiness I feel, nothing in life looks better. The dull, conservative ways I was taught by my parents and my college profs have no attraction for me. So I decide to return to Dallas and try my luck at another bar.

Searching all over Dallas for Ken, who still has my things but no longer lives in the duplex, I finally locate him. But the first thing he tells me is that I owe him money—$300—for leaving him stranded. He has moved my stuff into a storage unit and will show me where it is once I give him his money.

Reluctantly I fork out the cash, only to find out, to my horror, that Ken has given away all my possessions. He had fallen behind on the rent at the duplex, even when I lived with him, and the landlord evicted him. Ken took only his own things and left all mine with the landlord, who probably sold or gave them all away. I am so furious with Ken that I get violent, messing up his apartment—and him—before leaving.

Ken's irresponsibility and my own stupidity at trusting him with my things really cost me. I have lost a $10,000 stereo system, five crates full of records, two full sets of china, a pile of clothes, and a number of personal valuables. All I have left is a few outfits and several pairs of shoes.

I start a new job as DJ at Noto's, a small restaurant/bar on Dallas's north side. I get the job because some of my old bar friends work here. I have picked up a lot of DJ skills from living with Ken, and my track record in the bar business is good.

As in my past positions, I do my job well and am soon given supervisory responsibility over the other employees. I devise several Monday-night promotions that push us ahead of the other clubs in the area. One is called "Bar Wars," in which employees of other restaurants and bars are invited to compete for prizes and free drinks; the other is a casino football game for regular customers. Both receive rave reviews, and we begin to pack the house on Monday night, which is typically the slowest night of the week. Before long, Monday actually becomes our biggest money-making night.

Business grows until Noto's gains a reputation as *the* hot spot in North Dallas. I receive several more promotions and salary raises, until I am one of the highest-paid employees of the parent corporation. With my fat paychecks I am able to expand my drug dealing in the Dallas area. My friend Don moves to town and we become partners again. Again, life seems as good as it has been in recent memory—maybe even as good as it can ever be.

Thirteen

"The Scum of the Earth"

*DJ-ing at Noto's on Friday, January 13, 1984, and
feeling good. The place is filling up, the music pul-
sates throughout, and more people move
onto the dance floor.*

I watch all the action from my perch in the sound
booth. It has *not* been an unlucky day for me; I
have sold a few sizable quantities of cocaine
during the day and am carrying a big wad of cash in my
pocket—around $10,000, in fact. I rarely carry this
much money around with me, but I haven't yet had a
chance to transfer it to a safe place.

I notice two girls coming toward me and recognize
them as recent customers of Don's. Since we had both
met them one night at the club, and Don sold them a
couple of grams, I assume that's why they're coming to

me. Don and I have a policy of not selling snow to each other's customers, but as the girls walk up and ask me for some stuff, I notice that Don has already left, so I agree to perform the transaction.

I ask the girls to step into the sound booth where it's dark. The first one hands me a $100 bill, and I give her a gram of coke in a small plastic baggie. Then she steps outside, while I sell the second girl one-half of a gram. She gives me three $20 bills and nonchalantly says, "Keep the change." These words strike me as odd, because my experience has been that people don't just give their money away, especially drug money. But I don't worry—Don has sold to these girls before and nothing happened, so it must be safe.

"Hey, thanks," I say as she leaves the booth. Then I turn to the mike and announce the next record. Feeling a little tired, I decide to wake myself up with a couple of hits in the back bathroom.

I am totally unprepared for what I see when I step out of the sound booth. Six men are pointing guns at me. "Police!" one of them shouts. "Hit the ground face down—you are under arrest for possession and delivery of cocaine!" Before I even have a chance to figure out what is happening, they grab me and throw me to the floor. One of them holds me down, while a second handcuffs me behind my back and a third shoves my head down with his boot. I cringe at the pain.

"You don't even deserve the nice treatment we're giving you," the officer who cuffed me snarls. "You are nothing but the scum of the earth."

As I lie there pinned to the floor for several long, humiliating minutes, a thousand thoughts race through my head: *What is going to happen to me? Will I lose my job? What about my condo? My car? My possessions? How can I warn Don? What are they going to do*

Kregel found God again — in the cooler

Jon Kregel learned that white powder leads to trouble.

By Chris Meehan
Press Religion Editor

Jon Kregel had just handed the attractive woman a couple grams of cocaine when six police officers appeared from out of nowhere.

Guns drawn, the police threw Kregel to the floor of the north Dal-las bar in which he was working, jammed his hands into cuffs and told him he was under arrest.

"They weren't too nice. They threatened to blow my head off. They called me the scum of the ————l who was in

caine and sentenced to 25 years at the Texas Department of Correc-tions.

Prison was rough. He got into fights and twice had to spend 90 days in solitary confinement. But prison also brought about his salva-tion.

Before going in, he was a lost soul, hooked on a white powder, he tells audiences across the country.

"I don't know what would have happened if I hadn't gone to pris-on," said Kregel, nephew of Robert Kregel, owner of Kregel Publica-——— 733 Wealthy St. SE. "I realize ————— ———tion."

cocaine, he said he had been living a fast-paced, totally secular life. He drove fancy cars, wore expensive clothes, dated fast women and had no God other than himself. "I was into the night life, into making the big bucks," he said.

In jail, however, he discovered a book he had put down several years before when he was a student at the Grand Rapids School of Bible and Music. That book was the Bi-ble.

Behind bars, the drug dealer turned into an evangelist when he started to read about a faith he had turned his back on soon after he left Grand Rapids in the early 1970s to play professional soccer in New York.

He rediscovered, he said, the God he had first met as a youth growing up in Barcelona, Spain. "I found a God who loved me, a God who gave his only son so people like me can live, so I could be born again," he said.

In jail, he grew in faith and prom-ised God he'd change his ways once he was released.

After two years in prison, Kregel appealed his case.

He'd never been in trouble be-fore so the judge reduced his sen-tence, making him eligible for early last year for parole.

"God's grace was working in my life," he said. "As soon as I got out, I knew the Lord was calling me to minister to kids, to tell them about the dangers of drugs."

Kregel was paroled just over a year ago to a halfway house in year ago ———— then he has

er," he added. "Yet through it all, the Lord has given me a second chance. God does answer prayer."

Kregel is the son of Harold and Esther Kregel, who adopted him when he was 4 and living in an or-phanage in Marburg, West Ger-many. The Kregels served as mis-sionaries in Spain for 31 years and returned to this country about six years ago.

"We're so glad that there's been this change in Jon's life, that the Lord is opening up so many doors of service for him," said Harold Kregel, vice president of publish-ing for Kregel Publications.

It was after high school in Spain that Jon Kregel decided to attend the Grand Rapids School of Bible and Music. At GRSBM he played and coached soccer, a sport that he learned in high school. And after he left college, he signed on with the New York Cosmos, a profes-sional soccer team.

For four years he played soccer, then he moved to Indianapolis, where he studied nursing and end-ed up working as a nurse in hospi-tal emergency rooms.

That career lasted a few years and then he went to Texas, where he got into the bar business and eventually became a drug dealer. Throughout this time, he had littl contact with his family.

"One of my favorite books of th Bible now is the Book of Jonah. / every move, at every turn, he ke going down until he ended up the belly of the whale at the botto of the sea," Kregel said.

His own journey was down, fr ———————dent to professi

to me? Am I going to jail? Will they be easy or hard on me?

But at that moment the invincible Jon, the guy who knows how to talk his way out of anything, can do absolutely nothing. Helpless and heartbroken, I realize that no one is coming to my rescue. I have to face this one on my own.

While I sit on a barstool in the sound booth, my arms locked behind me, a husky man in a brown suit reads me my rights. I stare blankly at his badge, not hearing a word he says. My mind keeps wandering. I keep hoping that I'll wake up from this nightmare and that everything will be fine. The officer jerks me back to reality by tugging at my handcuffs, which bite at my wrists and cut off the circulation. "Do you understand your rights?" he asks. The record I put on is still playing. I nod.

After parading me through the club in my handcuffs, the police take me into the lobby and sit me down on a couch. Customers coming in the front door stare at me as they pass; I bow my head in humiliation and look at my feet. A couple of my friends walk in, and I try to duck my head behind the officer guarding me. I am so embarrassed and ashamed that I ask the cop if he'll take me out to the parking lot or somewhere else where I won't be seen.

"Shut up," he snaps back. "You don't have any rights now—we'll take you out when we're good and ready."

Funny how, only a few minutes ago, I was virtually in charge here, breezing through the crowd, talking with friends, doing DJ duty. My biggest worry was over which girl to see after work. Now the tables have turned, and everything looks different.

A moment later the record ends, and an eerie quiet

settles over the club. No one is there to keep the music going. A giant lump rises in my throat, and my heart pounds. The cuffs are really hurting now. More fears and questions streak through my mind: *Who should I call with my one phone call? Will the police close the club because of this bust? And if they do, will the club owners try to sue me? What is jail going to be like? What will my parents do if they find out about this? How can I get rid of the coke I still have in my shirt pocket?*

Finally I am escorted out of Noto's by no less than five policemen and into the back seat of an unmarked police car, a brown Dodge. The car speeds off, and a plainclothes detective brusquely begins to search me. Shadows from the street lights pass over his older, wrinkled face as he first removes my wallet and checkbook. Then he mutters, "Do you have any more cocaine on your person?"

There is nothing I can do but answer him honestly. "Yes, sir, I do—inside my shirt pocket." Quickly he throws his right arm across my shoulders, pinning me to the seat, and with his left hand removes the three baggies of white powder from my shirt. I feel like a little kid getting caught with his hand in the cookie jar—except now I'm going to be spending the rest of my life "in my room."

Immediately the detective fires question after question at me, without waiting for me to answer: "Where did you get this cocaine? Do you have any more at home? Do you realize how much trouble you are in? Where do you live? How long have you been dealing drugs?"

Only one of these questions registers, and it haunts me: "Do you realize how much trouble you're in?" The lump returns to my throat, and a tear falls to my suede jacket. As I discover that I am being taken directly to the county jail in Addison, my fears now shift to what I will experience there. I have heard stories from people who have been to jail and have watched countless drug busts on TV, but somehow I always remained detached, never once thinking it could happen to me.

The car pulls into the well-lit driveway of a one-story red building with no windows. A steel garage door rises, then closes behind us. Bright floodlights bathe the garage. Outside the car, I am accompanied through several more sets of security doors, which clang shut as we pass. Down a long gray corridor to the cells we walk. No one speaks; the only sound is of heels tapping the tile floor. Each step takes me further and further away from freedom. At the end of the hall, the officer waves to a closed-circuit TV camera and one last set of double doors opens.

Now I'm seeing a prison close up for the first time. We pass a row of cells on the way to the admitting area. They are small, gloomy, and dirty. At the far end of each cell, two steel slabs, painted bright yellow, jut from the wall and serve as beds. On each slab is what looks like a swollen piece of gray cardboard, which apparently qualifies as a mattress. A matching gray blanket—actually a tattered piece of cloth—rests at the foot of the beds.

Opposite the beds, a stripped-down steel toilet protrudes from the concrete floor. I notice armies of roaches encamped along the walls, unconcerned about our presence. Rather than bars, a small steel door with a half-inch Plexiglas window seals each cubicle. The doors have a slot at the bottom for slipping meal trays back and forth. More closed-circuit cameras monitor every possible move a prisoner can make.

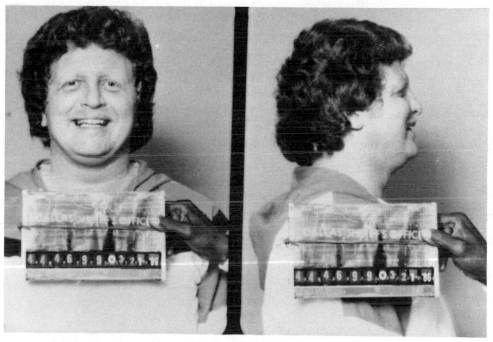

"Mug shots."

I shudder at this sight. It begins to sink in that this hole is about to become my new home, possibly for a very long time.

Going through the degrading admissions procedures, my wrists and hands are now so swollen from the cuffs that they hurt even when I breathe. A corrections officer finally removes them, much to my relief, and then says, "Okay, stand over here, empty all your pockets, and then remove all your clothes." I stand there for a moment, trying to rub the circulation back into my wrists.

"C'mon, we don't have all night!" another officer barks. "Get those pockets emptied and get them fancy drug-dealing clothes off your body. You ain't gonna need those clothes where you're going." It occurs to me that he is referring to the state penitentiary. *Is it really possible that I'll be sent there?* I have heard that the penitentiary is ten times as terrifying as this county jail. *What will happen to me there?* I shiver at the possibilities.

Slowly I remove my wallet, my checkbook, and my watch and put them on the counter. Then I dig the fat wad of money from my front pocket and lay it down. A gleam appears in the officer's eyes as he looks first at the money, then at me. Quickly he snatches it up and slaps me across the face with it. He counts it out loud with glee, stacking it into neat piles of a thousand across the counter.

"Ten thousand dollars," he sneers. "An awful lot of money for a kid walking around town. Plan on doing some grocery shopping later?" He chuckles at his remark, then glares at me. "The state will be taking all of this money as evidence," he declares sternly, "and we will be filing a lien on this money to pay for the long-term investigation we have had on you."

Trembling at his words, I continue to disrobe, down to my undershorts and finally—on his order—down to nothing. *Where are all my friends now that I really need them?* I think. *Nowhere to be found. I guess it just comes down to me, standing here naked in this cold room.* Several other men hustle in and out of the room with paperwork. My height and weight are taken, I am inspected for any identifiable tattoos or scars, and all kinds of additional information are recorded. Finally one guy rifles through my clothes, then throws them back at me. "Okay, get dressed and come over here for pictures."

I hold up a card with a long number on it, and the flash of an old Polaroid camera fires twice—for a straight-on and a right profile shot. Then I am escorted to a small dark room with two bare desks and a few old wooden chairs. A man's voice says, "Come on in. Sit down." As my eyes adjust to the darkness, I see a man in blue nylon athletic pants and a white T-shirt. And in the shadows I see two other faces—faces I recognize. They are the two girls with whom I made my last cocaine sale tonight.

I'm feeling terribly afraid as I face interrogation. The man in the athletic pants breaks the silence. "I am Lieutenant Mark Johnson, narcotics division. I can be your best friend or your worst enemy. If you cooperate with us and help us, we will go easy on you in court. If not, you are in for some serious trouble."

He reads me my rights, then continues: "You know that you are under arrest for four counts of felony cocaine sales and two counts of felony possession of cocaine. Each count carries five to ninety-nine years in the Texas Department of Corrections. Buddy, you are looking at a bunch of time. You know that, don't you?"

"Yes, sir," I reply, my voice quivering.

Again he assures me that if I help, he will talk to the judge and ask for leniency on my behalf. Then he starts into his questions. First, "Where do you get your cocaine?"

I remain silent, wondering what to say. *Should I spill my guts and tell everything I know, or should I keep my mouth shut? Will they really be easier on me if I talk, or are they just trying to trick me into giving them information?*

"Who are you trying to protect?" he asks, bearing down on me. "We've busted your whole ring, including your partner, Don."

So they got Don, too. Suddenly a hundred faces of

people I have dealt coke with flash into my mind. I wonder which one of them has talked. *Who has betrayed me? Who do I blame?* As I consider whether to protect any of them or "plead the fifth" and wait to talk to my attorney, I break out into a sweat.

Before I can decide what to tell my interrogator, he curtly dismisses me: "Looks like this one isn't gonna help us at all. Make sure he gets the worst. Get him out of my sight." I shiver in fear as an officer steps in, grabs me by the arm, and takes me back to the front desk. I am fingerprinted, then escorted to my cell. By now it is around midnight. A horrid, sinking feeling comes over me as I duck through the steel door, turn, and watch it bolt shut behind me.

Fourteen

Filling the Lonely Void

Transferring to the Dallas County Jail. I am awak-
ened at five on the morning after my arrest and
told to "get ready" for the transfer.

Since I have nothing with me, I wonder what I'm supposed to do to get ready. Soon a few guards arrive. They handcuff me, put shackles around my ankles, and help me into the back of a van, which takes me downtown into Dallas. All over again I must submit to the same humiliating check-in procedures.

Later that morning I am taken to a courtroom for a bond hearing. I sit next to five other guys and wait to face the judge. One of the guys was arrested for molesting a child; another for burglary; another for attempted murder; another for drunk driving (he had slammed into a car and nearly killed someone); and another for drug dealing. My first thought is, *Oh, no—I'm going to a jail full of derelicts.* Then it occurs to me: *But what, really, is the difference between me and them?*

Out of the six of us, my bond is set the highest, at nearly half a million dollars. Since I have no money—all of my possessions and assets have been confiscated—I realize I'll have to stay in jail until my court date. Certainly no one will show up here to help me, and anyone I know who can actually afford to put up my bail will probably be arrested out of sheer suspicion. Again it strikes me how shallow and fleeting my friendships have been. I feel lonely and afraid.

I am assigned to the seventh floor of the Lew Sterrett Jail, E tank, cell A. My work detail is to serve in the kitchen as a cook, which I don't mind since I've had so much experience working in restaurants.

Trying to survive in jail until my court date, which isn't for six months, I do my best to learn the official rules of the place so as not to get into trouble. Even more difficult to learn are the unwritten rules—the ones that keep a person from getting hurt or killed. For example: Don't raise a fuss about anything. Don't argue with anyone. Don't get involved in any disturbance, even if you're trying to help someone who's being unfairly treated. Don't ask questions. And so on.

One Saturday morning a few weeks after arriving in jail, I witness a brutal fight between a white guy and a black guy, all over how loud to turn the television. The black guy likes watching "Soul Train" in the day room and cranks up the volume pretty loud. The white guy, who wants quiet, gets up and turns it down to nearly a whisper. They go back and forth, the volume rises and falls, and words are exchanged. The rest of us in the room say nothing—we just wait for the inevitable clash.

Sure enough, they square off and lunge at each other. The fight ends in a matter of moments, but not before major bodily damage occurs. The black guy lies motionless on the floor after having his head crushed against the bars. The white guy bleeds from numerous gashes on his face and body—inflicted by the black guy's long, carefully sharpened fingernails. All over how loud to keep the television.

I'm coming down from my cocaine addiction. Since my arrest, I have more or less had a constant craving for the stuff. On bad or especially depressing days, the desire grows more intense. Of course, this parallels the way I used cocaine in the past—to feel better on a bad day, to escape from my emptiness, to gain the approval of friends.

At first, I am so caught up in adjusting to my new environment, convincing myself that I am really in jail and not dreaming, that I am able to ignore the cravings. Unfortunately, they don't go away; they return, again and again. To my surprise, I hear through the prison grapevine that I can get coke if I want it, though it's difficult and risky. But when I am offered some eventually, something in me manages to refuse. Maybe it is because I have come nearly full circle and experienced the miserable consequences of using the stuff. Or maybe it is just because I don't want to be caught and get into worse trouble than I am already.

But my craving continues, and withdrawal symptoms set in, mostly in the form of occasional tremors—the "shakes," and cold sweats. Usually, when I feel the symptoms coming on, I quickly ask to go to the recreation area, where I run furiously, play ball, or lift weights until the tremors subside.

At one point, a new inmate is placed in our "tank,"

still coming down from a trip. He has been injecting coke for some time (known as "running blow") and also taking "speed balls" (a mixture of coke and speed). He looks nearly as bad as my late friend Ed: bloodshot, bulging eyes and nerves totally out of control. He lies on his bed, shaking violently. Then he begins to throw up, but he is so weak he can't get up. He simply lies in his own vomit, only to throw up again minutes later. No one comes to help him. I am horrified at the sight. But it occurs to me that I could very well be in his place; I have been on the same road.

Fortunately, at the time of my arrest my addiction had not yet reached the desperate level of this guy—and therefore my withdrawal isn't as severe. I almost always snorted my cocaine and occasionally smoked or "freebased" it. Though I've always known that ingesting coke in any form is unhealthy and even dangerous, I could never bring myself to use a needle. Now, as I watch this hundred-pound skeleton writhe on the bed, I see a picture of what I could have become, or what I can still become if I return to coke.

Sitting in my cell, evening after evening, I wonder how I can deal with my lonely, empty self without cocaine. The coke is out of my system now (though the craving will probably always remain), but I have nothing to replace it with. And my friends—where are they? I haven't had even one visitor here in jail. All my life I have depended on friends to give me a good feeling about myself. If my friends thought I was great, I *was* great. But now they're all gone. As I look into myself, I wonder if there is any of me left—or at least anything in me that is worth holding on to.

For some reason, my parents come to mind. I wonder what they would think if they knew where I am now. I haven't spoken or written to them in several years, figuring they wouldn't be able to handle my being in the bar business. I reflect on the values they taught my sister Karen and me. My feelings are mixed. I believe Mom and Dad had good values and cultivated them in us kids. But I also think they made some mistakes. As a young kid, abandoned by my natural parents and coming from an unstable life in the orphanage, I badly needed vast amounts of attention and assurance—probably more than any average set of parents could give.

Mom and Dad, however, needed to devote countless hours to *Librería Evangélica*, the Christian bookstore they opened when I was thirteen years old, and to their church activities, to the point that I felt ignored or even neglected at times. The bookstore was the first Christian bookstore in Spain and they probably underestimated the time and energy needed to develop and manage the store. It seemed that the only times I *did* get their attention were when I had gotten into trouble. On those occasions, unfortunately, I felt more of their judgment and disapproval than I felt their love. So, as I grew up, I gradually turned my back on them and their values—and their God. Instead, I looked for other ways to find acceptance and approval: through sports, through impressing friends, through drugs. But where did it get me? Temporary, superficial acceptance at best, and ultimately free room and board in this jail. And I still feel empty. Now I clearly see that it's been me, not them, with the real problem.

A question pops into my head: *Just because I thought my parents weren't there for me as much as I needed, does that mean I should have rejected their values? Is it possible that in my anger I closed myself off from the good values they wanted me to live by? And how could they help if all I ever did was lie and steal?*

In spite of the mistakes my parents made—or that I *think* they made—I always knew they loved me and that they brought me up the best way they knew how. And I've always known that they had a sense of purpose, an underlying foundation in their lives. They talked to me about it many times as I grew up, but somehow it never clicked before. Their foundation, they told me, was in their relationship to God and to Jesus Christ, as taught in the Bible. That primary relationship, they said, gives fulfillment and purpose to everything else in life.

A foundation, I think. If there's anything I need right now, that's it. Maybe I should take another look at a Bible.

I remember someone telling me when I first got into jail that if I requested a Bible, the prison chaplain would visit me on a one-time basis. So I fill out the request form, thinking, *Hey, why not? I never get any visitors anyway—certainly a meeting with the chaplain won't hurt.*

Nearly a week later I am called for my visit with the chaplain. We are locked in a small room, where we talk for a few minutes. I quickly tell him about my background, my missionary parents, the Cosmos, getting into drugs, and so on. Mostly he listens, asking a question here and there. He closes with a brief prayer and then says to me: "Jon, you already know that this Bible contains the Truth, and that it will bring you the happiness you seek. Now it's time for you to read it, believe it and allow yourself to be set free." Then he leaves me, and I return to my cell with my Bible.

I stare at that Bible, which rests—closed—at the end of my concrete bed. The past few days since the chaplain gave it to me have been the loneliest days of my life. Something in me resists opening this book. Maybe it's that I think it will judge me and give me a long list of do's and don'ts. Or maybe it's because I know that reading it might lead me to make a major shift in the direction of my life, and I'm afraid of that, too.

Finally, one day after kitchen duty I decide to start reading. I follow the chaplain's advice and open to the Book of John in the New Testament. Being a missionary kid, I am no stranger to the Bible. I've read it plenty of times, memorized passages, even taken courses on it in college. But in spite of all my reading while growing up, something never "clicked."

As I begin chapter 3 in John, I read about a guy by the name of Nicodemus, who visits Jesus one night to ask what he must do to enter the kingdom of God. Jesus tells Nicodemus that he needs to be "born anew," undoubtedly a strange concept for Nicodemus to understand. But then Jesus clarifies what he means with a simple statement, one that I have read a thousand times: "For God so loved the world that he gave his only begotten Son, that whoever believes in him shall not perish but have eternal life" (John 3:16).

Something finally clicks.

For the first time, I see this verse in a whole new way. I've always read it with the emphasis on *perish*— "You'll go to hell if you don't believe." But now it looks so positive, more like an invitation to live fully and have hope by believing in Jesus.

As I sit there on my bed, another verse I remember from long ago pops into my mind: "What good is it for a man to gain the whole world, yet forfeit his soul?" I realize that in the past ten years I *have* "had it all" in many ways. I've been a nationally known soccer star.

I've made more money than some people will make in a lifetime. And I've experienced nearly every imaginable kind of pleasure, whether from parties, women, or drugs. And yet a void always remained—the void in my soul. I wonder, *Is it possible that Jesus Christ is the only one who can fill it?*

I consider what it would take to allow Jesus to enter that empty space in me. I feel as if I need to let go of something first. But what? Though I think of all the terrible and raunchy things I've done and feel deep remorse, I realize that behind those awful deeds lay an *attitude,* one that I must now set aside. It is that feeling of invincibility, the false belief that I can beat anybody, that I can make it on my own, and that I don't need anybody else, even God. I have nurtured this feeling in myself, this pride, ever since junior high. Now I sense that it's time to let go of it.

I kneel next to my concrete bed and pray for the first time in many years. "Jesus," I say, "please forgive me for running from you for so long." My tears begin to flow. "I am so sorry for all the sins I've committed against you. Please forgive me. And please come in and fill that lonely place inside of me."

A feeling of gratefulness wells up in me. "Thank you, God, for giving me this second chance in life. And thank you for my parents and for my sister Karen. Make the circumstances right some time for me to talk to them and see them again. Please help me to serve you with all my strength, now and when I get out of jail."

Kneeling there in a cold jail cell in my underwear, I feel a sense of freedom, true freedom, for the first time in my life. Again the tears flow, but this time they are tears of happiness and joy. I have made a decision, a choice, to let Christ have control of my life. I have taken the first step into a whole new way of living.

I am so excited that I want to tell someone what has happened to me. Quickly I get up and describe the whole experience to the guy in the cell next to me. He thinks I'm nuts, but I don't care.

Fifteen

Unwritten Rules

Knowing that I still must go to court and receive
my jail sentence. No matter what happens, I'm
sure I'll have to do some time.

Somehow the prospect of a few years in jail doesn't terrify me like it did before, because now I feel a sense of purpose. I can put that time in prison to good use, by studying the Bible, growing in my faith, and sharing God's great news with the other prisoners.

As my court date approaches, I know that I can reduce my sentence by revealing the names of my drug connections to the police. I have already been informed of the opportunity for a plea bargain. But I have seen too much during my years in the drug scene. If someone gets caught and gives out names, he dies—whether he's in prison or out. I don't want that to happen to me, especially now that I want to serve God with my life.

After prayer and reflection, I make my decision. I will accept whatever penalty I receive for my crime, but I will not give out any further information.

My court date finally arrives, nine months after I am arrested. My judge is Patrick McDowell, and I have prayed that he'll be lenient on me. Only one thing about my court appearance stands out—Judge McDowell's final words: "I hereby sentence you to twenty-five years of confinement in the Texas Department of Corrections. Good luck, son."

Twenty-five years! His words ring in my head for weeks. I can't understand why I receive such a harsh sentence. *How can God let this happen to me?* But I continue to read through the Bible, and a passage in the Book of Philippians gives me hope: "I can do everything through him [Christ] who gives me strength" (4:13). I try to accept that God does have a plan for me, and that he will help me get through whatever happens.

During the two-and-a-half hour bus ride to the Texas Department of Corrections, we're freezing. It is about 28 degrees outside, and the bus has no heat. Even worse, we wear nothing but a pair of coveralls with no sleeves or zippers and have no shoes or socks. We are so cold we throw away our food so we can wrap the lunch bags around our feet. We manage to do this only with great difficulty, since we are all handcuffed together and chained at the ankles. Once we do everything we can, we simply huddle together in silence and look out the bus windows. They have bars across them, but no glass.

First, for about a week we go to a diagnostic unit, where we are tested and prodded and then assigned to

Ellis II unit where Jon served his prison term.

various units across the state. I am sent to the Ellis II unit, located just outside of Huntsville.

Another bus delivers me and four other guys to Huntsville. As we round the curve, a giant complex looms before us, like a prisoner-of-war camp. There is an enormous, windowless building—three soccer fields long and two fields wide—surrounded by two rows of fencing, fifteen feet high, with barbed wire on top. Patrol towers anchor each corner of the grounds, with an armed guard carrying a high-power rifle.

As we proceed through the various gates and security checks, my heart sinks as I think of how long it will be before I leave this place. Yet, in my first few weeks here, I see various ways that God is taking care of me. For one thing, I am assigned to one of the "nicer" wings, the F2 wing, cell 113. And, while the other guys who came with me are issued jobs out in the fields, I am thankful to be assigned to kitchen duty again.

As I settle into the daily routine of my first year of prison life, I basically go about my business and don't really get involved with the other people. I work in the kitchen from 2:00 A.M. to 10:00 A.M., then return to my cell and stay there most of the day to study the Bible.

When I am promoted to cook in the officers' mess hall, however, I begin to come out of my shell. I make a number of friends and get to know some of the officers. I share with them what has happened in my life and tell them about my dream of starting a ministry to young people about the dangers of drug use. They listen with interest and talk to me about their lives as well. As their cook, I often prepare special dishes for them at their request, and we enjoy a good working relationship.

Positive experiences like these make life in jail a lot more tolerable. Unfortunately, no matter how hard you try to stay out of trouble, things do not always go your way in jail.

I spend a month in solitary confinement—for saving a guy's life. One day as I arrive at the mess hall for work, I hear shouting from the kitchen. I walk through the door, only to find myself in the middle of a stand-off between an inmate and one of the guards. The inmate is waving a paring knife and shouting threats.

Trying to stay calm, I look at the inmate and say, "C'mon, just turn in the knife before you make things worse for yourself." Suddenly the guy lunges at me with the knife. I dodge him and grab his arm to keep him from stabbing me. After we struggle for a moment, the guard finally jumps in and we manage to secure the knife. The inmate is taken away and placed in isolation.

Oddly, I am called before a kangaroo court to "defend" my actions. I can hardly believe my ears when they tell me I am charged with carrying a contraband weapon. "But I just walked into it," I protest. "I never had any intention of getting involved!"

They respond by sentencing me to thirty days in solitary. There's nothing I can do. At first I shrug my shoulders, thinking thirty days isn't all that bad. But then I see what solitary is like. I'm placed in a tiny, bare, tiled room, hardly big enough to stretch out in. Other than a crude steel toilet, there is no bed, no furniture; in fact, there is no light. I am permitted to bring two things with me: my Bible and my boxer shorts. For the next thirty days, I cannot shower or shave. All I can do is lie on my back on the floor, reading my Bible by the hall light that seeps through the crack in the door.

Though the conditions are far from comfortable, I make the best of it and actually come to enjoy the long block of time I can spend reading and talking to God. At the end of the month, I return to my regular cell and my job, and things continue as they did before.

By now I have learned my lesson and stick by the unwritten rules of prison, even as I watch terrible violence occur. I stay away from all disruptions, no matter what. One memorable morning we are awakened at four, the usual time for breakfast. Though today is my day off (I'm normally at work by two), I decide to get up and have breakfast for a change.

As I stand in the chow line, I notice some commotion further up the line. Four guys are verbally maligning another inmate—over what, I don't know. Shortly they begin shoving, then landing blows. This time I do nothing but stand back and observe in silence.

The four guys quickly gang up on the poor victim, punching him and then beating him mercilessly with their stainless-steel food trays. By the time guards arrive, the guy lies dead on the floor, his skull smashed. As they carry him off, no one says a word. Then we all go back to our business.

Next I experience a raid from the Goon Squad for the first time. One morning after I get off work, I drop into bed and fall asleep almost immediately. Normally I am a light sleeper, because in jail there are always noises—cell doors clanging, people yelling—that prevent you from sleeping soundly. On this particular day, I happen to be in a deep sleep.

The next thing I know, a man grabs my sheet and tears it off me. "Goon Squad! What are you doing still in bed?" he yells.

Jolted out of sleep by a bunch of strangers, I rear up instinctively and raise my fist. This is a mistake. Immediately two other guys jump me, yelling and swearing. Having no idea what is going on, I fight back, trying to defend myself. Finally I am thrown to the concrete floor and cuffed. I emerge, fortunately, with nothing worse than a few bruised ribs, cuts and scrapes.

Later I find out that this Goon Squad is a team employed by the warden to perform *blitzkrieg* searches of the cells, looking for drugs or any kind of contraband. Normal procedure when they strike is to get up, step out of your cell when the door is opened, and wait until you're cleared to return. Somehow I must have missed that portion of orientation. For my automatic defensive response, I am granted another thirty days of solitary.

I must overcome various obstacles to go to church each week. In jail, attempting to do anything other than exactly what someone orders you gets very complicated. To attend chapel services, which are held in the evening, I must either have a special pass or simply wait until the guards announce the activity. Herein lies the problem.

Most of the guards couldn't care less about what activities are going on or whether they allow you to leave. Half the time they conveniently "forget" to announce chapel, and I end up missing it. Even more frustrating is that chapel occurs at exactly the same time as the evening "count," when the guards must justify exactly where every prisoner is. If a guard happens to be nice enough to allow me to go to chapel, he must count me ahead of time and then search me when I leave and when I return. The hassle is so great that only a few guards do anything to help me get to chapel. But I persevere and manage to keep contact with a few guards who respect my desire to attend.

As I walk to the chapel one evening, a passing guard says, "Hey, here comes the Bible fairy—how sweet." I have never been called a fairy before, and with all the hassle I must undergo to make it to chapel, I am infuriated by his words. If ever I want to hurt someone, it is him. Somehow I restrain myself, but it takes me a long time to forgive his wisecrack.

Sixteen

Free at Last!

Nearly two years go by as I continue my cooking job, keep up my good behavior, and avoid getting caught in the middle of others' scuffles. It begins to occur to me that I might be able to do something to shorten my prison term.

I spend some time doing research in the law library and learn that I can ask my attorney to file a motion in Judge McDowell's court for a sentence reduction based on good behavior and plans to begin a new ministry. After completing all the paperwork, I breathe a prayer as I drop it in the mail: *God, please have this motion approved if it is your will.*

Reflecting on the people I've been closest to in jail, I especially single out several of the cellmates I have over time. One of them, Ted, an ex-biker, has already served sixteen years for murder and assumes he'll never get out. He maintains that rough-and-tough, Harley Davidson image, but at night when the lights go out, he drops his mask and reveals to me the deep hurt in his life. He was sexually abused as a child, ran away from home at a fairly young age, and got in with the wrong crowd. Alcohol and drugs got the best of him. I listen to him and try to encourage him by sharing what God has done in my life.

Another cellmate, John Moody (real name), has become a Christian, and we spend hours and hours talking about the Bible, helping each other memorize Scripture passages, and praying together. When his prison term is over, he doesn't want to leave because he enjoys our fellowship so much. I am sad to see him go.

Mark, my last cellmate, is a big guy of over six feet who walks with a limp. Shortly after his arrival, I come back from work and notice that half of his leg is standing next to the bed. He wears a prosthesis, he explains, because he lost part of his leg in a gun battle.

Actively involved in the drug scene, Mark had gone to a party. Suddenly the door had broken down and a SWAT team of armed police raided the place. He grabbed an UZI machine gun and, without bothering to aim, sprayed bullets at the cops. By the time he had emptied the gun, he had killed several police and wounded a few others. He had also been shot up in one leg.

Mark had received six consecutive life sentences for the incident. His injured leg developed gangrene and had to be amputated. Thus the prosthesis. Like many of the other men I talk to, Mark is also hurting inside. I am able to tell him about Jesus, but I never really know how he responds.

Probably the one man who has the greatest impact on

me in prison is Chaplain John Larson. He loves God, cares deeply for the inmates, and spends many hours talking and listening to them. Whenever I get together with him, he seems to have an encouraging word, and he directs me to Bible passages that give me hope and help. We study the Scripture together, along with some of my other Christian friends—Wayne, Randy, Lazaro, and others.

Receiving some legal mail, which I must go and sign for, I am very excited when I see it is from my attorney. I tear open the envelope, remembering that it has been about three months since I first sent him the paperwork for the sentence reduction.

I read the letter. It says that the motion was heard by the judge—and *passed.* My heart leaps as I read that my twenty-five-year sentence has been reduced to only five years! And since I have already served three years, I should be eligible for parole in a matter of months. I can hardly contain my joy, and I rush to tell my friends.

I meet the parole man for the first time in December 1986, knowing he has a reputation for being imposing, impersonal, and insensitive. I look forward to seeing him with a mixture of excitement and fear. When I am called, I walk down a long hallway into a dark gray waiting room. Ten guys are in line ahead of me, and I stand for three hours as each person is interviewed. I am the last one.

Hesitantly I step into his office and sit down. Opposite me he sits, the feared parole man, a large guy in his mid-forties. He asks me lots of questions, makes a few notes, and gives me the opportunity to talk. I begin to tell him about how I have changed since I decided to follow Christ and allowed him to control my life. He listens, stonefaced, then asks a few more questions. Back and forth we go for nearly two hours, but I have no sense of whether I should feel hopeful or discouraged. He finally scribbles down a few more notes and curtly dismisses me.

I meet with him two more times in the weeks that follow. At our second appointment, he asks, "Where do you want to go once you get out?"

"Well, I'm not really sure," I reply. "I have no home."

"Well, come up with a parole plan and present it to me at our next meeting."

So I do some thinking and prepare my parole plan, which basically amounts to a statement that includes the name and address of someone I'll be staying with so the parole people can verify my location once I get out. I wish that I had some Christian friends in the area that I could live with, but I know no one. So I end up giving the name and address of an old friend I knew back in the bar business—someone I know will put me up when I am released. This plan is approved at my last meeting with the parole man.

One weekend, a church group from Tyler, Texas, comes in and conducts a seminar on the Christian life. I enjoy the workshop and talk with them afterward about my situation. They tell me that if I need a place to stay, they'll be happy to help me any way they can. I find myself drawn to these Christian friends. *If only I had met them a few weeks earlier when I needed a name and address,* I say to myself.

Now I don't know what to do. When I explain to the parole people that I want to change my parole plan, they tell me that any changes in the paperwork cause an automatic ninety-day delay, possibly extending as long as six months. One thing I know for sure is that I don't want to stay in jail for a minute longer than I have to.

So, for the next few days, I pray to God: *If you want me to go to Tyler, please do whatever is needed to make it possible.* Then I present my request to the parole people, explaining that I want to go to Tyler only if I can do so without additional delays.

It is March 18, 1987, and I am sitting outside in the recreation area, relaxing after my work shift. The sun is shining, but the temperature is a bit cool. I close my eyes and rest.

Soon I hear my name being called by one of the women guards. I pretend not to hear, thinking that perhaps I'm being called back in to work, which happens sometimes. But she keeps calling and finally walks right up to me. Looking at the gym I.D. number on my pants, she says, "Number 437370. Are you Jon Kregel?"

Weary-eyed, I nod yes, waiting for the inevitable order to work extra hours. Instead, she smiles at me and says, "Jon, if you want to, you may get ready to go home now."

Home! I can hardly believe what I'm hearing. I jump to my feet and take off for my cell. In a matter of minutes, I pack up the few books I have acquired and ready myself for the release procedures. Three other inmates and I are escorted to a small holding cell, where we wait for a while. Then we are ushered onto the same bus I rode into this place three years ago. It all happens so fast that I don't even see my friends to tell them good-bye. But I know they understand—most prison releases are conducted in this fashion.

The bus first takes us to another unit on the compound, where again we must wait in a holding cell and endure all kinds of final administrative procedures. Altogether, 111 of us are being released today, to various points around the state. Several more hours pass as, one by one, we trade in our prison clothes for civilian "circus" clothes. I receive a pair of bright blue pants, a red shirt, and $200 cash.

Finally, after signing our names about forty times, we are each issued our places of parole. Out of the over one hundred being released, I am the only one paroled to the halfway house in Tyler, Texas.

The prison bus drops us off in the quiet downtown streets of Huntsville at about seven o'clock that evening, nearly eight hours after the guard first approached me with the good news. I am now a free man. The first thing I do is stop in my tracks and thank God for what he taught me in jail, and most of all for allowing me to get out. I walk down to the bus station to board my bus for Tyler.

Seventeen

A Clean Break

Feeling excited as I go into the station to buy my
ticket. I look on a map to find out just where Tyler
is. The city, which has about 100,000 people, is
100 miles east of Dallas, and slightly south.

I discover that the bus doesn't leave until 12:30 A.M., so I walk around Huntsville to kill a few hours. As I return to the bus station, a couple of guys emerge from the next-door bar, drunk and noisy. I recognize them as two of the men who had just been released from jail. As I stand there watching them, a police car pulls up and takes them away. *On their way back to prison already, and they never even made it out of town,* I think.

Now, while the bus makes its way through the dark night to Tyler, I am thankful that God has allowed me to take my life in a different direction. I am making a clean break from my past and will soon settle into a new home, new friends, and new surroundings.

At 4:30 A.M., the bus finally pulls into the station in Tyler. I get off, grab my two boxes of books, and then wonder what to do next. It is so early that I hesitate to call anyone, but I decide to dial the number of the halfway house anyway. A man answers and tells me he's just leaving for work, so he'll be glad to stop by and pick me up.

About twenty minutes later, a blue pickup pulls in front of the station and stops right next to me. The guy flings open the passenger door and says, "Howdy—jump in!"

Somewhat perplexed, I ask him, "How do you know I'm the guy you're looking for?"

He takes one long look at me and laughs. "Well, the circus sure ain't in town, or else they left you behind!" *(Oh, yeah—my clothes.)*

The guy weaves through town and turns into a gravel parking lot behind a large house. "Here you are," he says, "this is your stop. Go on inside and find Bill—he'll fill you in on all the details." I thank him for the ride, take my books, and make my way into the house.

"Mr. Bill," as everyone calls him, is a tall, slender man with silver hair and cowboy boots. He has a friendly air about him. He knows where I've come from and asks a few questions about my time in prison. Then he gives me a copy of the house rules and directs me to a bunk in a back room. Since I have been up all night—I didn't sleep one minute on the bus—I plop right onto the bed and fall asleep.

Almost immediately, I hear Mr. Bill's voice again. "Okay, everyone, it's five-thirty. Time to get up! Breakfast is on!" Several other guys moan and complain, but Mr. Bill goes around and makes sure everyone is up and getting ready for breakfast. Even me.

I thought people got up this early only in prison, I mumble to myself, rolling out of bed. Shortly we are all sitting around a big table—actually a big board on top of a pool table—eating breakfast. I go right back to bed afterward and sleep until mid-afternoon. The bed, I notice with a smile, has springs and a real mattress.

When I finally wake up, I call some of the Christian friends from Tyler I had met that weekend in jail: Richard and Karen Longenecker, Jeff and Paula Walker, Bill Peel, Cecil Price, and June Lininger. They seem thrilled to hear from me and tell me they've been praying for me.

These friends, who hardly know me, rally to provide me with all kinds of help and support. One of them supplies me with a job opportunity painting houses. Another invites me over regularly for delicious home-cooked meals. The others give me friendship and fellowship as I have never experienced before—a startling contrast to the shallow friendships of my past. I share with all of them my hopes for starting a ministry, and they promise to help in any way they can.

Standing up in front of a hundred people, I give a public account of God's work in my life for the first time. Bethel Church, where all my new friends attend, has asked me to speak, and I am very nervous. I worry that people will hear my knees knocking over the microphone.

I stumble through my story the best I can, the nervousness diminishing as I go along. I talk about growing up in Spain, Pele and the Cosmos, getting into the drug scene, and how I met God in jail. Again I describe my dream of setting up a ministry to tell young people about the dangers of drugs and the freedom of knowing God. By the time I finish, a sense of joy and excitement has swept over me. After the service, many people come up to me and volunteer to help.

One couple, Ray and Diane, invites me to their house for dinner that week. They ask me: "Jon, what do you need right now to get your ministry started?"

"Well, to be honest," I say, "right now I really need a car."

Within a few days Ray calls. "Jon—Diane and I would like to give you an old Honda Civic we're not using. It runs a little rough, but I think it'll get you around okay."

When I take a look at the tiny, forlorn vehicle, I see that the paint is flaking from the hot Texas sun, and it has a flat tire. It is a far cry from the luxury sports cars I drove during my drug-dealing days. But I am so grateful for Ray's and Diane's help that I don't care. I fix the flat, wipe down and wax the body, and put that Honda right on the road.

A few weeks go by, and I am able to save up enough money to buy some clothes and a pair of sneakers. My next step is to find an inexpensive apartment, my own place. First, I secure permission from the parole office to move out of the halfway house. Then I locate a small flat on the south side of town with a low rent, but I can't afford the security deposit. To my surprise and deep gratitude, the Longeneckers offer to cover it.

Moving day is hardly an ordeal. The stuff I have to transport consists of only three outfits, two pairs of shoes, and two boxes of books. It takes me all of an hour. As yet I have no furniture, and my voice echoes off of the bare walls, but I am happy. God is providing for me a little at a time.

Before long I take a better-paying job in a furniture

warehouse, which I discover is the most strenuous work I have ever experienced. We lug giant boxes and crates of furniture around, and sometimes must stack them three and four units high. At the end of my first week there, my back hurts so badly I can't bend over. But somehow I get used to the muscle-work and make enough money to buy a few pieces of furniture for the apartment. More friends generously donate a bed, a dining room set, kitchen items, and linens. I feel that I am on my way to getting reestablished so I can proceed with my ministry.

I talk to my parents for the first time in more than four years. It is Father's Day, 1987, and I am eating lunch with Gary and Linda Lesniewski, a couple from church. Linda asks, "So, Jon, are you going to give your dad a call today?"

"Well, I really would like to," I reply, "but—they don't know anything about what's happened to me with jail and all, and I'm afraid of what they'll say. Besides, I think they're in Spain."

"But he *is* your father," Linda persists. "He deserves to know where you are. And you have some very good news to tell him, too."

Finally she convinces me to call. I go into the bedroom and stare at the phone. I am already beginning to sweat from fear and nervousness. *I really do want to talk to Mom and Dad,* I think, *but what will they say? How will they respond?* Most of all, I wonder whether they will still love me. I quickly pray that God will prepare them for my call, and then I dial their number.

No answer.

I'm tempted to leave it at that and report to Gary and Linda that no one was home. Actually, I'm not even sure my parents still live at this number, the last one I had for them in Spain. But I figure that since I've already decided to go through with the call, I might as well try to locate them.

I call my Uncle Bob in Grand Rapids to ask him. Aunt Betty answers and is shocked to hear my voice. She is even more shocked when I tell her I have just been released from prison. My parents are temporarily in Illinois, she says, and Dad is speaking in a small church there. I take down the number and tell her I'll catch up with them later.

Again I breathe a prayer as I dial. My stomach hurts, and I am sweating all over. The call goes through quicker than I expect, and someone answers on the first ring. It is a gentle, woman's voice, one that I don't recognize.

"Uh, is Harold Kregel there?" I say, without identifying myself.

"Just a minute, please," says the voice. I hear commotion in the background; apparently several people are in the room. Fifteen seconds of waiting feels like forever. Finally I hear footsteps coming toward the phone, and then the clack of the receiver being picked up.

"Hello?" It is Dad's familiar voice.

I hesitate, not knowing what to say. Then I blurt out: "Hello, Dad? This is your son, Jon—I wanted to let you know that I'm alive and to wish you a happy Father's Day."

I hear him gasp, then shout across the room: "Mummy, come quick—our son is on the phone!" Mom picks up the extension and says, "Jon, is it really you? Are you okay?"

Tearfully I begin to tell them how I messed up my life and went to jail, and how God took hold of me. But I don't get very far before we are all crying. It feels so good to hear my parents' voices again. They assure me that they still love me and that they have been so worried about me. They tell me they even hired a detective to look for me at one point.

I am so emotionally drained that I find it hard to talk for very long. But, as I say good-bye, I feel I've at least taken the first step toward reconciling with my family. I thank God for making this phone call happen.

The ministry is getting under way. Several churches in the area invite me to speak, with a favorable response. I appear on a local radio talk show, then a local TV broadcast. With each of these opportunities, I feel God's confirmation of my ministry hopes.

Later, when I speak at Allied Baptist Church in Longview, Texas, I meet a wonderful couple, Jack and Joyce Henry, and their daughters Jackie, Heather, and Rebecca. Joyce had heard me on the radio, and initiated the church's invitation for me to speak. Afterward, she and Jack invite me to their home for dinner.

Jack has an interesting background. Years ago he had been a delivery man in the food business, and his boss taught him how to steal food from grocery stores! But then Jack became a Christian and decided he wanted to live his life differently. First, he paid back all the grocers he had stolen from. Then he began to conduct seminars for the food-and-grocery industry on how to prevent theft—based on his own experience. Jack's seminars were very well received and eventually became quite lucrative for him. Now he feels God wants him to give some of the money he has made to other Christians who are trying to make a difference in this world. That's why he wanted to talk to me.

The Henrys take a special interest in me and my ministry, and they offer to help me in several major ways. First, Jack pays my way to take several months of public-speaking instruction in Dallas during the evenings. The training helps me a great deal. Yet, even as I learn, it is still difficult for me to make contacts and build the ministry while working full-time. At this point I have returned to painting houses and am logging fifty- and sixty-hour work weeks. I yearn for an opportunity to make the ministry my full-time occupation.

Jack knows this, too, and decides he wants to help me in a second major way. One day, he sits me down in the office he has built behind his house and says, "Jon, I really believe in what you're doing and that God has called you into the ministry you're pursuing. I think you need to be devoting all your time to this. If you're willing, I'd like you to work full-time right here out of my office, and I'll pay you weekly. You don't need to do anything for me—just use whatever you need here to get your ministry off the ground."

Jack's invitation moves me deeply. I look around his office at the typewriter, computer, photocopier, and telephone he is so graciously making available to me. Since he travels extensively, his office sits empty much of the time, and I can put it to good use. *Now, finally, I can really reach out full-time to all the people out there who are hurting,* I think. Enthusiastically and very gratefully, I agree to his proposal and hang up my painting overalls for good.

In this new office, I begin by developing some printed materials to use in promotion. Whenever the opportunity arises, I go out and speak. At first, I must still obtain permission from the parole office any time I leave town. But my parole officer, Linda Baab, "happens" to be a Christian and gives complete support to the ministry. Soon I am able to travel freely, with no restrictions, and I visit churches and youth groups in Virginia, Connecticut, and Michigan. The ministry is beginning to grow. I meet an interesting Christian lady and we begin dating regularly.

Eighteen

So Much to Share . . .

Gazing out the airplane window on a flight from Dallas to Grand Rapids. I am about to see my parents for the first time in several years.

*A*few weeks after our Father's Day conversation, Mom and Dad offer to fly me to Michigan for a long weekend, so they can catch up on all that has happened to me. I really want to see my parents, but I am so nervous about all the questions they are likely to ask that I feel sick to my stomach for the entire flight. I keep worrying: *Will they be mad at me or will they welcome me? Will they ask for details I don't want to divulge? I wonder how they will respond when I tell them about the drug scene, about my sexual escapades, about being in jail.*

When the plane lands, I wait until nearly all the passengers have gotten off before I get up from my seat. Finally I muster up the nerve, and I make my way off the plane and down the long ramp into the terminal. My legs are shaking.

As I pass through the terminal door and look around, I behold two sets of loving eyes waiting anxiously for me. Mom and Dad walk right up and throw their arms around me. Tears of happiness and relief come to my eyes.

During the half-hour ride home, I decide to take the lead in the conversation. I ask if they would mind just listening for a while as I attempt to describe what I have been doing for the past few years. Then, after I finish, they can ask all the questions they want. We arrive home in what seems like an instant, and I continue my story there. Mom and Dad follow up with only a few questions that evening. Before turning in for the night, we all pray together, thanking God through our tears for taking care of us and bringing us back together. I am emotionally exhausted, but very happy.

I wonder how my son, Jeffrey, is doing. He is now eight years old, yet I haven't spoken to him in six years. I feel deep remorse over having left him, especially with so little further contact. Over the years I realize that I've hurt many people—Jeff, Peggy, my parents, and others. Sadly I realize that I can't go back and undo all that I've done. I have no choice but to accept the consequences of my past actions and do my best to make wiser choices from now on.

Still, I think about Jeff. My parents tell me Peggy still lives in Indianapolis and has remarried and that Jeff has been legally adopted by her new husband. I don't know their exact address, but I pray that before long God will give me the chance to see my son again. I left him under such terrible circumstances. When the time is right, I plan to ask him to forgive me, tell him how much I love him, and ask if we can get to know each other again.

I've been out of jail almost two and a half years. Linda and I have gotten married. The ministry is growing rapidly.

But now I'd like to share my concern for a former cellmate of mine, John Moody.* John's parents were divorced when he was young. His father is an alcoholic who once took his son along with him on a burglary. The pair was caught. John took the blame and his father was released.

But that's only the beginning of John's troubles. He served four or five jail terms for disorderly conduct, intoxication, and one for theft. When I met him he had about five months left to serve on a drunk and disorderly charge coupled with possession of a concealed firearm.

John had committed his life to the Lord. We spent a lot of time in Bible study together and attended chapel. He would buy things for me because I didn't have any money. John was released about six months before I was. Before he left, I told him I loved him like a brother and asked him to stay in touch.

About a year after my release I see these headlines in the Tyler paper: *Ex-TDC Inmate Arrested for Capital Murder.* I am shocked to read of John's new troubles. Two weeks later I visit him in a small county jail in Abilene. I wait for him in a small room. Suddenly the door opens, John comes in and starts crying. I hug him and ask him what happened.

*This name has not been changed.

John began, "When I left jail I was on fire for the Lord. I read my Bible. I prayed. Soon I started a lawn service business and became quite successful. Now that I look back on it, that was probably the worst thing that could happen. I stopped reading my Bible and forgot about the Lord. Soon I turned my back on him.

"One day some friends asked me to drink with them. I had had a bad day. I lost a couple of accounts. I was depressed. So I started drinking with them. I drank a six-pack of beer. It tasted so-o-o good! I just continued drinking. After that I smoked a couple of joints. I remember one of my friends coming up and saying he had a gift for me. (I had gotten married but didn't have rings for my wife so I asked my friends to be on the lookout for a nice wedding-ring set.) My friend gave me the rings without telling me how he got them.

"The next hour and a half are a complete blank to me. The only thing I remember is going to a friend's house and falling asleep on his porch.

"Some police came and shook me awake. They had been called by neighbors to remove a drunk. I was taken to jail for public intoxication. There I was fingerprinted and told to empty all my pockets. In one of my pockets were the rings—later identified as being taken from a woman who had been murdered in her home. The police checked the home and grounds for fingerprints and found, among other prints, some that possibly were mine. Not surprising, because this woman was one of my lawn-service clients. Based on my past record of four or five convictions and the incriminating fingerprints, I was charged with capital murder."

John's story shocks me, especially when I remember the depth of his commitment to God. I see how easy it is to walk away from God. And I also see John's remorse. . . . He insists he did not commit the murder and I believe him. I also believe his resolve to renew his relationship with God and decide to help John in any way that I can.

I attend John's four-day trial in February 1989. His mom sits on my left; his dad on my right. I serve as a character witness for him, but because of my previous record I am promptly and severely "discredited" by the district attorney. The evidence appears mostly circumstantial but John has a "record" and cannot establish exactly what he was doing at the time of the crime. The jury's verdict is *guilty.* The next day John is returned to court to hear the sentence: *death penalty.*

So John is transferred to death row and now awaits execution. He has become reconciled to God and his desire now is to serve God to the best of his ability for as long as he is allowed to live on earth. His lawyers are still going through the various processes of appeal, but if they don't succeed, John will be executed within three years. I visit with him and write letters encouraging him to remain steadfast in the faith, and send him devotional materials.

I continue to receive almost daily confirmation from God about my speaking ministry. One day Mom calls and tells me about Doug*, a guy in their church recently arrested for drug dealing. I take down his number and give him a call. His mother answers and hesitates to let me speak with him. He's out on bail awaiting sentencing. But, after I explain who I am and why I'm calling, she reluctantly allows it.

To my surprise, Doug tells me, "I already know who you are, Jon. But first let me give you a little background about myself." His voice sounds fairly light and hopeful, and I wonder why.

---

*This name has not been changed.

He proceeds to tell me about his life. I say very little—mostly I listen. He attended Christian schools from elementary through high school. In high school he started drinking out of curiosity, but soon began to get drunk regularly.

After high school, Doug worked at several jobs, and eventually began managing a local health club. He became the top salesperson of club memberships and began to make more and more money. As his paycheck grew, he spent more and more late nights at the bar. His life got wilder, and his quest for wealth increased.

One day a man offered him a nice sum of cash to deliver a package. Doug agreed—and soon found himself making many such deliveries and raking in the money. Though he knew he was delivering cocaine, he didn't care at first because the money was so good. As the deals got bigger, however, the pressure increased and his paranoia grew.

Meanwhile, Doug's drinking problem worsened as he used alcohol to ease the tension. After having way too much alcohol one night, he took a joy ride in his new Mazda RX-7. The next thing he knew, he awoke in the intensive care unit of the hospital. He was told he had hit ten trees at a hundred miles an hour, rolled the car over five times, and landed in a ravine. Besides several broken ribs, a cracked pelvis, and internal damage, he needed more than a thousand stitches and had to have his spleen removed.

Lying in the hospital's ICU, Doug cried out to God for forgiveness and healing. He survived with no major side effects—only a giant scar. But even this close call did not lead him to stop his alcohol-and-drug activity. He soon forgot God's miraculous healing in his life and resumed his usual business. Finally it happened—the police caught and cornered Doug almost the same way they got me. And Doug is headed for jail, like I was.

As I listen to Doug tell me his story, I marvel at how similar it sounds to my experience. Then he says to me: "As I sat in my cell, Jon, I thought of you. A few months before I was arrested, I had heard you speak at Calvary Church during Christmas. You told about how the drug world had controlled you, and how you were able to turn your life around by turning your life over to God. At that moment I knew you were speaking to me. Yet, afterward, I still refused to put my life in God's hands. So I ended up learning the hard way.

"As I thought about what you said that day in church, I knew what I had to do. There, in jail, I swallowed my pride, bowed my head, and asked God to take charge of my life. Since then, Jon, I've had the chance to tell others about what it took for God to get my attention. Now, even though I've lost all my possessions and am facing up to twenty years in a federal penitentiary, I am filled with joy at the opportunity to serve God with my life."

Doug pauses, and tears well up in my eyes. Quietly I thank God for using a messed-up life such as mine to help Doug.

I spend many hours with Doug, his wife, Colleen*, and their parents. We're all a great encouragement to each other. I thank God that I am able to talk to many others like Doug who have gotten involved with drugs and alcohol.

Traveling around the country I share my story in high schools, colleges, and churches. I have developed two main seminars—one for young people and another for adults. When I speak to high school and college students, my talk is titled, "Values, Drugs, and You." I urge young people to think about three questions: What

*This name has not been changed.

are your values? Where do they come from? What are they based on?

Then I tell them about my life, from Spain to Bible school, to pro soccer, to the drug scene, to jail, where I finally decided to turn my life around. I explain that in spite of my missionary background and Bible-school training, I had never established a solid foundation for making my own choices. Not until I met God in that lonely jail cell did I finally choose to turn my life over to him, and allow him and his word to be my foundation.

I usually close my talk by encouraging students to stay away from drugs, to keep thinking about those three questions, and—most importantly—to lay a strong biblical foundation in their lives so they can make the right choices for their future.

For adults and parents, I call my talk "What You Need to Know to Say No." I provide a variety of background information on the primary causes and effects of drug use among young people. I explain that, for many kids, avoiding drugs isn't always a simple matter of "just saying no." Many factors play into a young person's decision to use drugs, one of the most important being the quality of that person's home life. Only as parents and concerned adults maintain a loving, yet firm, presence in their children's lives will those youngsters have the inner security and strength to resist the pressure to use drugs. Finally, I give some practical tips on what parents can do to improve their home environment and help their kids make positive choices.

How urgently we need to help young people make smart choices early on and stay away from drugs! From my own experience, and from that of so many I've talked to, I am becoming more and more convinced that

Jon, speaking at a
school assembly in
Ashland, Kentucky
(1989).

most people don't decide all of a sudden to become involved with drugs. Wrong decisions often start with rather insignificant consequences, usually as a result of peer pressure in high school or college, as it did with me.

I wanted to be liked and accepted by my friends so badly that I would do almost anything. For me, drugs became the way to make friends and to be popular. But, as my life story shows, drugs made my life more and more empty, more and more chaotic, more and more dangerous. They ended up alienating me from everything that really mattered—from my family, from my own self, and from God.

If God hadn't touched me that day in my jail cell, I'm not sure I would be alive today. And if I were alive *without God*, I would most likely still be rotting away in some federal penitentiary. I pray that God will somehow use my story to help others avoid the terrible mistakes I made. More importantly, I pray that others who don't yet know the joy and fulfillment of knowing God will be moved by my story to seek him in the Scriptures and in a local church. I am so thankful that he has given me a second chance. Accept him as your Savior and Lord and he will change you, too.

If you'd like to contact me about a personal problem or to make arrangements to speak at a group meeting, I can be reached at Jon Kregel Ministries, P.O. Box 131480, Tyler, TX 75713. Phone (214) 759-9667. Ask for a tape recording of my testimony and other pertinent information. I hope to have a video cassette of one of my speaking engagements available after June, 1990.